I0764209

DOESTICKS AND HIS FRIENDS.

NEW YORK:
EDWARD LIVERMORE,
20 BEEKMAN STREET.

1855.

Press of Geo. C. Rand, 20 Beekman St.

R. CRAIGHEAD, PRINTER AND STEREOTYPER,
53 *Vesey Street, N. Y.*

THIS IS NEITHER

A HISTORY, ROMANCE, LIFE-DRAMA, BIOGRAPHY,

AUTOBIOGRAPHY,

NOR

POST MORTEM EXAMINATION,

BUT A SERIES OF

**Unpremeditated Literary Extravaganzas,**

WRITTEN WITHOUT MALICE AFORETHOUGHT

BY THE SINGLE HERO THEREOF,

PURELY FOR HIS OWN GLORIFICATION,

AND PRINTED BY THE PUBLISHER

SOLELY FOR HIS OWN PROFIT.

# Nothing.

---

In a literary point of view this book claims nothing:

This is the manufacturer's assertion.

In a literary point of view this book amounts to nothing.

This will be the reader's conclusion.

And if any skeptical person insists upon investigating the matter for himself, he will eventually be compelled to acknowledge the verity of this remark; and will, at the same time, bear a strong testimony to the sagacity of the publisher, who has put his trust in nothing—*for he will have bought the book.*

This work simply professes to be sketches of various persons, places, and events—some of which have been published, and some hav' n't; some are bad, and some are worse; but all have a claim to originality in treatment, although the same things may have been better said by better people.

Some of these bubbles have been, for some time, floating on the sea of literature—the lightest froth of the restless wave; still there are many of them which have never met the public eye, and which are here, for the first time, set afloat.

And for their publication the writer makes no apology. Accident has brought these "airy nothings" into notice; and although many of the thoughts are not novel in themselves, but are merely whimsically put, and not a few of the whims are borrowed unhesitatingly from others, they are dressed up in a lingual garb so quaint, eccentric, fantastic, or extravagant, that each lender would be sadly puzzled to know his own.

It is undoubtedly this trick of phrase, this affectation of a new-found style, which has caused their widespread newspaper notoriety. And in the hope that people will buy the book before the trick is stale, and not suspect the secret of the joke until they read it on this page, the writer has authorized the collection of these roving unsubstantial ink-brats into their present shelter, and now presents the whole uncouth family for inspection, trusting that the experiment will "put money in the purse," not only of himself, but of his sanguine publisher.

This book, like Hodge's razors, was "made to sell;" and if the sometime good-natured world will pay the price, and have its huge grim smile over these unlicked fancies—although in a political, moral, or utilitarian sense it will have gained nothing—it will, in a literal if not literary view, lose nothing.

But if it is in a surly mood, and chooses to look with dignified contempt upon this avowed and candid literary humbug, some one will be disappointed to think he has miscalculated the fickle taste of the aforesaid world and some one will be out of pocket by its sulky humor; but *of* these persons, their whereabouts, their circumstances, or their names, the world can *say* nothing, because it will know nothing; no, nothing.

Q. K. PHILANDER DOESTICKS, P. B.

NEW YORK, *June*, 1855.

# Table of Contents.

# What He Says.

---

## I.

### How Doesticks came to think of it.

IT is not pretended that this volume is a work of inspiration, or that any portion of it has been revealed by accommodating "Spirits" through the "Medium" of those crack-brained masculine women, or addle-headed feminine men who profess to act as go-betweens from Earth to the Spirit World.

No part of it has been "rapped" out by uneasy tables, or thumped out by dancing chairs; Doctor Franklin didn't dictate it; Lord Byron didn't write it; Napoleon wasn't consulted about it; Cardinal Richelieu didn't have a finger in it; George the Third hadn't anything to do with it; Shakspeare didn't suggest anything in it; and Benedict Arnold didn't know anything about it.

That these worthies might have afforded much valuable information, offered many important improvements, and enriched the book with a host of wise opinions, had some sapient "Medium" asked their assistance, is unquestionable. But as neither Andrew Jackson Davis, or any other spiritual call-boy was at the elbow of the writer to summon these desirable but defunct individuals, they were probably left to pursue, in unmolested peace, their favorite and dignified occupations of "tipping" tables, knocking on partitions, drumming on floors, frightening old women and little girls into hysterics, and upsetting the propriety of whole parlors full of furniture, whole closets full of glass-ware, and whole cup-boards full of pots, pans and other kitchen gear. For in such intellectual and elevated employments are great men's ghosts engaged, when they pass into a more refined state of existence, if we may credit the assertions of the self-styled "*Spiritualists.*"

But, unassisted, and alone, I, the writer, have undertaken this mighty work, instigated only by the Spirits hereinafter referred to, and by the representations of my publisher.

Although at present neither celebrated nor notorious, I have a presentiment that I am speedily about to become one or the other. Through an accidental rip in the curtain of futurity, I have caught a glimpse of the Goddess of Fame. I have heard her sing out from her rather elevated position for me to come up and take a "hasty plate" of glory; and I have not the heart to refuse the request of such a good-looking female, preferred in such elegant language. I am going to shin up the slippery rope leading to her aerial temple (for accurate dimensions and appearance, see engraving in the old Elementary Spelling Book), for the purpose of taking a hand in the game of literary renown, trusting that Nature has given me trumps enough to make the "game," and that Fortune will deal me all "the honors."

For weeks I have been haunted perpetually by a voice—not a "still, small voice"—but a large voice, a considerable voice· a voice vociferous, unctuous, and ever-present, and withal insinuating, and not wholly distasteful. It has been constant in my ear, suggesting pleasing hopes and fanciful desires; and though its *notes* were often varied, yet ever was the *theme* the same; and the constant burden of that ceaseless song was, "Write a book! write a book!"

And in dreams, too, visions of good-looking ladies with wings, came into my 7×9 chamber, and whispered in my ear, and they too said, "Write a book! write a book!"—and one I thought, with versicolored plumage, with her finger on her lip, quoted the perpetually murdered Shakspeare prophetically, and, no doubt, with an eye to the success of the volume aforesaid, and said, suiting with a fairy-like gesture the action to the word, "I could a tale unfold." And plucking a snowy quill, she gave it to me, murmuring, as did all the rest, "Write a book! write a book!"

Awoke—put on my pantaloons and boots, and in my shirt sleeves sat down to cogitate. Result is, that I shall use the lengthy quill—I shall accept the pressing invitation of the Goddess of Fame; and in order most effectually to *dis*-tinguish or *ex*-tinguish myself, hereby with malice aforethought, and the penalty of a failure before my eyes, I sit down to write a book.

But my physician informs me that I have got the "cacoethes scribendi," which he says is as bad as the small-pox, toothache, and yellow fever. The disease, he says, must have its course—it may end in a malignant biography—result in an infectious broadsword and blunderbuss, yellow covered novel, or degenerate into a weak form of pseudo-sentimental verse writing, in which latter case, on the appearance of the first symptom he intends to order me a literary tombstone.

Having fully determined upon making this literary effort, it became necessary to make up my mind as to what should be the contents of the work. A mental cogitation ensued. Philander was puzzled to know what Doesticks was going to write about—Philander asked Doesticks—whereupon Doesticks, in order to satisfy Philander, replied as follows, upon hearing which reply Philander was content.

## II.

### Doesticks satisfies Philander.

WHAT it will be all about, time alone will show, for although I have done a little of almost everything, it has in most instances been *so* little, that a premeditated autobiography would probably lack incident, and be deficient in interest. I have not as yet invented humbugs enough to earn a *Prince*-ly title, and not having made a fortune by ingenious trickery, metallic impudence and barefaced deception, cannot edify the " darling public, " by telling how the thing is done.

Never having made fierce love to a lady against her will, followed her from place to place in the small-beer spirit of presumptuous puppyism, been outwitted by her at last, and left to cool my amorous passion in a prison, the story of my courtship and its consequence, would not prove attractive.

As I have ever been on good terms with my

family, I feel no desire, under the guise of a fictitious narrative, to call any members of it miserly and mean, purse-proud and haughty, or to say that others are conceited, vain, selfish, silly, foppish, or weak-brained.

Novel writing is out of the question. I have tried that, but met with serious difficulties. I couldn't keep my hero of the same nation—in the first chapter I made him a Spaniard; two pages afterward he was an English nobleman; in the fourth chapter an Oriental juggler, balancing a bamboo ladder on his nose, and making a fig-tree grow out of the calf of his leg—and so on, successively, an Italian image-seller, a Dutch burgomaster, a South American Indian, and a Mississippi steamboat pilot.

I had as much difficulty in permanently locating the country of my fictitious favorite, as the Know-Nothing party of New York in the late election had, in determining the nativity of their candidate for Governor, whose chances of election were fair while he was thought to be an American, but who was finally defeated on the ground that he was a Hindoo, and owned stock in the car of Juggernaut. Poetry has been overdone; the gentle art has culminated in a recent "Spasmodic Tragedy," and in the sublime effusions of K. N. PEPPER, ESQ., whose matchless lays have won for him undying fame, and the admiration of several; and who so outruns competition that there is nothing left to be done in that direction.

In the play-writing vein, I have also failed; not from any lack of merit in my drama, as the manager solemnly assured me, but because he had not the menagerie requisite to its proper representation. Improving upon the hint offered by the managers of the "*Thespian Wigwam*," who have added an elephant and a circus company to their company of "gifted artists," I had introduced into my play a rhinoceros, a lioness, two hyenas, a team of "two-forty" reindeers, a couple of ostriches, and a muley-cow,—and even then there was but a slight obstacle —the manager might have procured the animals, but he was afraid the cow would quarrel with the rhinoceros, and so disturb the harmony of his establishment.

But this book, Philander, it will be impossible to class as strictly either classic, scientific, historical, humorous, or descriptive. Fantastic and extravagant it will be in many things; but we will do our best to make it agreeable to the palate of the public. I promise everything, like all book-makers, and I shall afterwards perform what is convenient, following the same reliable precedent.

My book shall be full of love and poetry to suit the "fast" young ladies, and shall be written in easy words of two syllables to meet the necessities of the "fast" young men.

I shall praise, flatter, and commend everybody and everything, that everyone may receive his meed of approbation; and I shall also censure, find fault, and criticise in an equally universal manner, that no one may escape his proper castigation.

I shall set forth a great multitude of fancies, theories, and hypotheses, that those who are fond of innovation may not lack gratification; and I shall immediately proceed to controvert and deny them all, that the conservative portion of community be not offended.

I shall cry down education and instruction, for there are those who consider all teaching an evil; and on the other hand, I shall advocate learning and science, for there is a very respectable minority which insist that the people may advantageously be taught something more.

I shall not stand up for love and charity, for it might induce people to love the wrong persons, and to give their pennies to imposters; and yet I shall not eulogize avarice and hate, for there are a few who think benevolence and kindness preferable even to these.

I shall not throw my influence in the scale of Protestantism lest the Catholics should take offence, nor yet shall strive to build up Catholicism, lest thereby the dislike of the Orthodoxy be incurred. Nor shall I show myself a partisan of religion of any kind, for the Atheist says it is all a farce. Neither shall I endeavor to inculcate principles of infidelity, for there is still an occasional prejudice in favor of Christianity.

It will be "a work which no gentleman's library should be without." It is considered necessary to the safety of the Union, that its democratic principles be thoroughly disseminated, and it is indispensable to the stability of the English throne that its monarchical doctrines be thoroughly comprehended. Every man, woman, child, canal driver, billiard marker, faro dealer, and member of Congress will be provided with a copy, thereby preserving the Union, destroying our liberties, and keeping unsullied the honor and dignity of "OUR FLAG."

I hope the public will be as well satisfied by this

eloquent speech as Philander was, that this book is one of immense utility, and will consequently peruse the same with a huge degree of gratification.

Doesticks on a Bender.

# III.

## Niagara.

I WAS never given to accepting the decisions of others as gospel in any cases where it was possible for me to manufacture a home-made opinion of my own; and I did not greatly wonder at myself when I discovered that my emotions, when I first beheld that great aqueous brag of universal Yankeedom, Niagara, were not of the stereotyped and generally-considered-to-be-necessary—sort. The letter which follows, and which is all the reminiscence of my visit extant, was published soon after, and extensively copied, and was, in fact, the first article which bore the name of Doesticks.

## IV.

## Doesticks on a Bender.

I HAVE been to Niagara—you know Niagara Falls—big rocks, water, foam, Table Rock, Indian curiosities, squaws, moccasins, stuffed snakes, rapids, wolves, Clifton House, suspension bridge, place where the water runs swift, the ladies faint, scream, and get the paint washed off their faces; where the aristocratic Indian ladies sit on the dirt and make little bags; where all the inhabitants swindle strangers; where the cars go in a hurry, the waiters are impudent, and all the small boys swear.

When I came in sight of the suspension bridge, I was vividly impressed with the idea that it was "some" bridge; in fact, a considerable curiosity, and a "considerable" bridge. Took a glass of beer and walked up to the Falls; another glass of beer and walked under the Falls; wanted another glass of beer, but couldn't get it; walked away from the

Falls, wet through, mad, triumphant, victorious; humbug! humbug! Sir, all humbug! except the dampness of everything, which is a moist certainty, and the cupidity of everybody, which is a diabolical fact, and the Indians and niggers everywhere, which is a satanic truth.

Another glass of beer— 'twas forthcoming—immediately—also another, all of which I drank. I then proceeded to drink a glass of beer; went over to the States, where I procured a glass of beer—went up-stairs, for which I paid a sixpence; over to Goat Island, for which I disbursed twenty-five cents; hired a guide, to whom I paid half a dollar—sneezed four times, at nine cents a sneeze—went up on the tower for a quarter of a dollar, and looked at the Falls—didn't feel sublime any; tried to, but couldn't; took some beer, and tried again, but failed—drank a glass of beer and began to feel better—thought the waters were sent for and were on a journey to the ——; thought the place below was one sea of beer—was going to jump down and get some; guide held me; sent him over to the hotel to get a glass of beer, while I tried to write some poetry—result as follows:

Oh thou (spray in one eye) awful, (small lobster

in one shoe,) sublime (both feet wet) master-piece of (what a lie) the Almighty! terrible and majestic art thou in thy tremendous might—awful (orful) to behold, (cramp in my right shoulder,) gigantic, huge and nice! Oh, thou that tumblest down and riseth up again in misty majesty to heaven—thou glorious parent of a thousand rainbows—what a huge, grand, awful, terrible, tremendous, infinite, old swindling humbug you are; what are you doing there, you rapids, you—you know you've tumbled over there, and can't get up again to save your puny existence; you make a great fuss, don't you?

Man came back with the beer, drank it to the last drop, and wished there had been a gallon more—walked out on a rock to the edge of the fall, woman on the shore very much frightened—I told her not to get excited if I fell over, as I would step right up again—it would not be much of a fall anyhow—got a glass of beer of a man, another of a woman, and another of two small boys with a pail—fifteen minutes elapsed, when I purchased some more of an Indian woman, and imbibed it through a straw; it wasn't good—had to get a glass of beer to take the taste out of my mouth; legs began to tangle up, effects of the spray in my eyes, got hungry and wanted something to eat—went into an eating-house, called for a plate of beans, when the plate brought the waiter in his hand. I took it, hung up my beef and beans on a nail, eat my hat, paid the dollar a nigger, and sided out on the step-walk, bought a boy of a glass of dog with a small beer and a neck on his tail, with a collar with a spot on the end—felt funny, sick—got some soda-water in a tin-cup, drank the cup and placed the soda on the counter, and paid for the money full of pocket—very bad headache; rubbed it against the lamp-post and then stumped along; station-house came along and said if I did not go straight he'd take me to the watchman—tried to oblige the station-house, very civil station-house, very—met a baby with an Irish woman and a wheelbarrow in it; couldn't get out of the way; she wouldn't walk on the sidewalk, but insisted on going on both sides of the street at once; tried to walk between her; consequence collision, awful, knocked out the wheelbarrow's nose, broke the Irish woman all to pieces, baby loose, court-house handy, took me to the constable, jury sat on me, and the jail said the magistrate must take me to the constable; objected; the dungeon put me into the darkest constable in the city; got out, and here I am, prepared to stick to my original opinion.

Niagara, non est excelsus (ego fui) humbug est! indignus admirationi!

# V.

## Seeking a Fortune—Rail Road Felicities.

YOUNG men in the west, when they get too lazy to plough, drive oxen, and dig potatoes, invariably either go to studying Law, Physic, or Divinity, or emigrate to New York to make their fortunes. Hence the inundation of two-and-sixpenny pettifoggers, the abundant crop of innocent-looking juvenile M. D's, and the army of weak-eyed preachers, whose original simplicity is too deeply rooted to be ever overgrown by the cares of after life. The portion of our country known as "the West" sends forth every year scores of these misguided innocents, who, had they stayed at home, might have grown up into tolerable farmers, or even been cultivated into respectable mechanics, but who, being once thrown into the whirl of city life, degenerate into puny clerks with not half salary enough to pay for their patent-leather boots.

It is a curious fact that two-thirds of the young

men from the country, their first year in the metropolis, do not receive as a remuneration for their valuable services a sum sufficient to keep them in theatre tickets.

If a committee of their employers should be detailed to investigate the hidden pecuniary fountain whence these young men obtain the funds many of them lavish so freely, the said committee would be considerably astonished to find out how much more champagne and oysters the N. Y. merchants pay for than the most knowing of them are aware of; and their wives would be astounded to learn how many bracelets and diamond pins had been presented to ladies of the theatre and ballet, and bought with their husbands' money. And many a country mother would mourn to hear that her darling had, in the first six months of his city life, learned to practise more vices than she had ever heard of, and among his other attainments, had acquired the elegant city accomplishment of spending his employer's money as freely as if it was his own.

And in due course of time the writer of this paragraph, wearied of the eternal sameness of a country village, the same unvarying prospect of ox-teams, hay-scales, errant swine, and wandering disconsolate cows, took the roving fever and resolved to visit Gotham, looking for a cure.

Packed up my traps in a red box, kissed all my friends who had clean faces, and bade a long farewell to the aspiring village (which had long since assumed the name of city, but had never grown large enough to fit the appellation, and for this reason always reminded me of a boy with his father's boots on,) where I had vegetated for several years; took a last look at its town-pump, its grocery, and its court-house square without any fence round it; feasted my eyes for the last time upon the dusty charms of the seminary girls who are perpetually going to the story-and-a-half post-office for letters which never come; rode to the railroad for the last time in the four-wheeled smoke-house, which, from early youth, had been impressed upon my ignorant simplicity as an omnibus; and taking my seat in the cars, left without many tears the town where I had treasured up such stores of classic knowledge under the consistent inattention of teachers who had been paid to neglect my education.

Paid the man with the brass door-plate on him, sixteen dollars and a half for a dirty piece of pasteboard,—hung up my carpet-bag on a hook which immediately broke down, and let the aforesaid bag drop on the bonnet of a populous lady with a pair of twins, whom it completely demolished for the time —settled myself in my seat for a comfortable nap—was continually roused therefrom by the door-plate man, who seemed to have a mania for inspecting the dirty pasteboard every fifteen minutes—got my mouth full of dust and cinders, which I converted into a mortar-bed in my stomach by drinking warm water from the spout of a water-pot (brought round by the boy who expects you to buy his greasy apples and ancient newspapers as a compensation for the temporary dilution)—changed cars about twenty times, and had the satisfaction of seeing my trunk pitched about by the vindictive baggage-men at every step, as if they were under obligations to knock it to pieces in the least possible space of time. (When it arrived at the end of my journey the lock was broken, the hinges pulled off, and a large hole punched in the end, so that I found my clean shirts full of gravel, and that a piece of brick which had got in through the place where the lock had been, had been rubbed against a daguerreotype of my lady-love, thereby demolishing her left eye and scratching the top of her head off.) Rode all night;

every time I would get into an uncomfortable doze the train would stop, more passengers come in, and I would have to vacate my seat to accommodate some woman with three children and a multitude of bundles (a woman in a railroad car always occupies four times as much room as she pays for, generally turning over the back of the seat next to her, and occupying one place for herself and the other three for her provisions and bandboxes)—then finding another place, and getting into an uneasy dream about earthquakes, wash-tubs, bass-drums, and threshing-machines, and waking up with a sudden choke when some unusually large cinder got into my mouth—coming to a sudden stop at some side station and finding my anatomical constituents in a most uncomfortable state of paralysis; my arms fast asleep and feeling like frozen sausages; my other extremities ditto, and with no more feeling in them than in a bass-wood log; having a dim consciousness that something was wrong, and endeavoring to navigate by means of the benumbed members before alluded to, and get out doors to see what the matter was, and in the attempt falling over the stove and knock ing my teeth out against the coal-hod—being called at four o'clock in the morning to assist in the dismal farce of breakfast, and sitting down (with my hat on and my hands dirty in order to be in the fashion) at a long table where the crockery looks as if it had not been washed in a month, and the only visible viands are cold biscuits, hard-boiled eggs, and despairing mutton-chops struggling inextricably in a tallowy ocean—where the half-awake waiters bring you apple-pie in place of coffee, and pour the hot water down your back, and spill the sugar in your hair—where, in the midst of your second mouthful, you are called upon to suspend operations and pay half a dollar to a man with uncombed hair who gives you wild-cat paper and crossed quarters in exchange for your Yankee gold—and where, before the third morsel reaches your expectant lips, the bell rings, the malicious engine gives its vicious shriek, and you are hurried, swindled and starving, into the cars again.

In this delectable manner for two days and nights I was hurried, hustled, and tumbled towards my journey's end—reached my destination at last, crossed the North River in one of those ferry-boats which run either end first like a crab, and on my arrival was instantly attacked by a crowd of runners, was forcibly thrust into a hack, the remains of my trunk tossed at my feet, and in obedience to my panting request, I was driven to that hotel, the cognomen whereof is simultaneously suggestive of holy men and of the adversary.

## VI.

### Seeing the Lions—Barnum's Museum.

AS soon as I had become comfortably established as a citizen of New York, and had replaced the straw hat with a green ribbon, which decorated my head at the time of my metropolitan advent, by a shining beaver with white fur on the under side; had run in debt for a new suit of clothes, and sold my trunk to buy a set of gold shirt-studs, I began to assume that knowing air of superiority which ever distinguishes the thorough-bred city man from his country cousins.

I made up my mind to devote the next six months of my valuable time, to seeing the sights, and becoming acquainted with the celebrities of the town. To this end I proposed to visit the various places of amusement, to go on excursions, join volunteer companies, run to fires, in short, to make myself ever-present, wherever there was anything to be seen, to which the verdant eyes of a backwoods Wolverine were unaccustomed.

I addressed myself a speech wherein I remarked, "Phil, you have now been a resident of this city long enough to know something of the localities thereto appertaining—know where the City Hall is—ditto Hospital. Also where the Astor House is generally located—can tell the general direction of Mercer and Bowery streets from the Crystal Palace—and can at most times of day point out Trinity Church with a tolerable degree of accuracy.

"But there are, nevertheless, sundry other points of interest, with which you should become familiar, and divers other objects whose names you should remember, that hereafter you may not mistake a Grand Street stage for a perambulating Circus wagon; or again, point out the Wall Street Ferry House to a friend and assure him it is the Hippodrome building, but be able after this to give reliable and correct information on these points to all who ask."

Accordingly, since that time, I have striven hard to acquire such a knowledge of the city that I could find any of the theatres without a Directory, and get home at any time of night without the escort of a Policeman.

Have been to the Battery, for which I paid a shilling to the dilapidated Hibernian who attends the iron portal—afterwards visited (by particular desire,) the cocked-hat shaped Sahara known as the "City Hall Square"—saw the splendid fountain with its symmetrical basin filled with golden fishes (as I was credibly informed)—I could not exactly perceive them myself—in the midst of its elegant miniature forest (yet in its infancy)—gazed with admiration at the ancient structure denominated the City Hall—said to have been built by the ancient Greeks, of which I have not the slightest doubt, as all the avenues leading thereto were thronged with *modern* Greeks, whose general costume was not so classically correct as I could have wished—looked at the glorious fountain which adorns the centre of the spacious lawn—admired the magnificent proportions of the vast forest trees which rear their lofty forms therein—gazed long and earnestly at the glittering jet (not quite so lofty as I had been led to suppose,) of the magnificent fountain which embellishes the princely grounds—then turned to look at a circular edifice, which, I confess, did not strike me as being remarkable for architectural beauty, but which undoubtedly is exceedingly useful—then turned to feast my wonderiı.g eyes upon the diamond-glittering drops of a fountain near at hand; looked with much approbation upon the wide and spacious avenues, and the clearly gravelled walks, and also at a fountain near by, which I think I have before mentioned; surveyed the other fine buildings near at hand, which adorn and beautify that triangular piece of earth; and ever returned with constantly increasing gratification to view a beautiful lake in the centre thereof, from the midst of which burst forth in aqueous glory the waters of a fountain; soon, convinced that I had seen my money's worth, prepared to leave—casting one longing, lingering look behind (as my friend L. E. G. Gray says,) at the glorious old classic ruin, the hall, and the pluvial splendors of the fountain.

Went out, but looking back, perceived that in the splendid park I had just left, there rose in "misty majesty" (vide somebody,) the jet of a fountain. Resolved to return and have another look at the ivied and crumbling ruins, and also to inspect minutely a fountain which I now perceived hard by.

Wishing to be perfectly *posted* up, I went to the *Post* office (the *Evening Post* office), and obtained a paper containing the latest news of the day, and also a list of entertainments for the evening. Desiring to see the Museum, of which I had read, and also to behold Barnum, of whom I had heard some mention, in connection, I think, with one Thomas Thumb, and Joice Heth, an antiquated and venerable lady, colored (who afterwards *died*), I determined instantly to visit that place of delectation, "perfectly regardless of expense."

Arrived at the door, man demanded a quarter, but, like Byron's Dream, "I had no further change," so was necessitated to get a bill broke; offered him Washtenaw, but that was too effectually *broke* to suit his purpose. Got in somehow, after a lengthy delay, and some internal profanity.

Soon after my entrance, young man, attired in a dress-coat, a huge standing collar, and a high hat, introduced himself as "A. Damphool, Esq.," gentleman of leisure, and man about town. Having never before had any experience of a class of individuals who compose, I am told, a large proportion of the masculine population of the city, I eagerly embraced the opportunity of making his acquaintance.

He also presented his friend "Mr. Bull Dogge," and we three then proceeded to view the curiosities; we commenced with the double-barreled nigger baby (which Bull Dogge says is an illegitimate devil),—

went on to the Rhinoceros (who is always provided with a horn, Barnum's temperance talk to the contrary nevertheless)—the Happy Family—the two-legged calf, (B. D. says it is not the only one in the city), a red darkey—a green Yankee—a white Irishman (Damphool says that this latter individual is an impossibility, and could only have originated with Barnum)—wax-figure of a tall man in a blue coat, with a star on his breast, (Damphool says it is a policeman, who was found when he was wanted; but Bull Dogge says there was never any such person, and that the whole story is a Gay fable,) found by the programme that it is supposed to represent Louis Napoleon; never knew before that he had one eye black, and one blue (Bull Dogge asserts that the usual custom is to have one eye both black *and* blue); wax model of the railroad man who swindled the community (now living on his money, and president of the Foreign Mission Society for the suppression of pilfering on the Foo-Foo Islands); wax figure of the abandoned, dissolute, and totally depraved woman, who filched half a loaf of bread to give her hungry children, and who was very properly sent to Blackwell's Island for it—also of the City

Contractor who *did* clean the streets—(Damphool states that he is residing at Utica).

Saw a great multitude of monkeys, streaked face, white face, black face, hairy face, bald face (Bull Dogge prefers the latter), with a great assortment of tails, differing in length, and varying as to color, long tails, short tails, stump tails, ring tails, wiry tails, curly tails, tails interesting and insinuating, tails indignant and uncompromising, big tails, little tails, bob tails, (Damphool suggests Robert narratives), and no tails (Bull Dogge says that some effeminate descendants of this latter class now promenade Broadway, and he swears that they have greatly degenerated in intelligence); pictures, paddles, pumpkins, carriages, corals, lava, boats, breeches, boa constrictors, shells, oars, snakes, toads, butterflies, lizards, bears, reptiles, reprobates, bugs, bulls, bells, bats, birds, petrifactions, putrefactions, model railroads, model churns, model gridirons, model artists, model babies, cockneys, cockades, cockroaches, cocktails, scalps, Thomashawks, Noah's ark, Paganini's fiddle, Old Grimes's coat, autocrats, autobiographies, autographs, chickens, cheeses, codfish, Shanghais, mud-turtles, alligators, moose, mermaids, hay-scales, scale armor, monsters, curiosities from

Rotterdam, Amsterdam, Beaverdam, Chow Sing, Tchinsing, Linsing, Lansing, Sing Sing, cubebs, cart wheels, mummies, heroes, poets, idiots, maniacs, benefactors, malefactors, pumps, porcupines and pill machines, all mingled, mixed, and conglomerated, like a Connecticut chowder, or the Jew soup of the Witches in Macbeth.

Upstairs at last, and into an adolescent theatre, christened a Lecture Room, (Damphool says it is known as the Deacon's Theatre, and that all his pious namesakes attend). Saw the play, laughed, cried, and felt good all over. Much pleased with a bit of fun originating in a jealous fireman, and terminating in a free fight.

Fireman Mose saw Rose, his sweetheart, with Joe, the hackman; got jealous, pitched into him—fun—thought of Tom Hood, and went off at half-cock—thus—

Enter Rose with Joe—sees Mose—Mose beaus Rose; Rose knows those beaux foes—Joe's bellicose—so's Mose—Mose blows Joe's nose—Joe's blows pose Mose—Rose Oh's—Mose hoes Joe's rows—Joe's blows chose Mose's nose—Mose shows Joe's nose blows—Joe's nose grows rose—Mose knows Joe's nose shows those blows—Joe goes—Mose crows.

Joe being whipped, and moreover being the only innocent one in the whole fight, was arrested by the vigilant and efficient police.

Damphool says that Joe treated the Emerald conservators of the public quiet, and is again at large.

Let Mose beware.

## VII.

# Model Boarding Houses.

IMMEDIATELY upon my arrival in the city of Newsboys and Three-cent Stages, I proceeded, as is hereinbefore mentioned, to the white-faced Hotel which is surmounted by the bird called Shanghai, who seems from the top of his lofty perch where he roosts in unreachable security, to crow over neighboring boroughs, and exult in the great glory of the Manhattan Island. It required, however, but a few days to weary of the "constant noise and confusion" of this saintly mansion, and to become sick of the eternal presence of men in white aprons who are everywhere at the same time, and who are, mathematically speaking, a constant quantity.

These waiters are certainly ubiquitous; at the table there is one at each elbow, at night a stranger is escorted to bed by a grand procession, and one pulls off his boots while another unbuttons his shirt-collar, and a third lights the gas and turns down the bed-clothes; a waiter meets you at the door, another takes away your overcoat and gives it to a waiter who presents you with a brass check for it—there are waiters in the bar, in the washroom, in the barber-shop, in the cellar, in the reading-room; waiters running races through the halls all night; there is always a snowy neckerchief and an outstretched palm when you leave the premises, and on sunshiny days there is invariably a distant glimpse of a white-jacket on the roof of the house.

As soon after my arrival as I could collect my senses, and knew enough not to take every M. P. for a foreign ambassador, and pull off my hat to the Star, I deemed it advisable to search for lodgings more quiet, and not so expensive.

It took about a fortnight to restore my mind to its accustomed serenity, and then having become, to a certain extent, a fixture in this high old town, it became necessary to search out a fit habitation, wherein I might eat, sleep, change my shirt (Damphool blushes), and attend to the other comforts of the external *homo*, and the inner individual.

My friend Bull Dogge having deserted his late place of residence, (on account of the perpetual reign of salt mackerel at the breakfast table), we started together on a voyage of discovery. To describe all the dilapidated gentlewomen, whose apartments we inspected—all the many inducements which were used to persuade us to take up our quarters in all sorts of musty smelling rooms, and to recount how many promises we made to " call again," would take too much time.

Suffice it to say, that at six o'clock in the evening, wearied out and desperate, we cast anchor in the domicile of an Irish lady with one eye. She assured us that her boarders were all " rispictible, and found their own tibaccy, and that there was divil a bug in the place."

We took adjoining rooms, and resignedly went down to tea.

I noticed that my cup had evidently sustained a compound comminuted fracture, and been patched up with putty (which came off in my tea)—that the bread was scant—the butter powerful—the tea, " on the contrary, quite the reverse,"—however, although matters looked somewhat discouraging—" hoping against hope"—we retired to our respective rooms.

Horror of horror ! ! O ! most horrible ! ! ! I was besieged—had I been Sebastopol itself I could not have been attacked with more vigor, or by more determined and bloodthirsty enemies.

For two hours I maintained a sanguinary combat with an odoriferous band of determined cannibal insects—armed only with a fire-shovel, I gallantly kept up the unequal conflict—but the treacherous implement broke at the critical moment; I thought I should be compelled to yield—despair filled all my senses—my heart failed me—my brain grew dizzy with horror—hurried thoughts of enemies unpardoned—of duties neglected—and of errors committed, rushed across my mind—a last thought of cherished home and absent friends was in my heart, and with a hasty prayer for mercy and forgiveness, was at the point of yielding, when my frantic eye caught sight of my cast-iron boot-jack. With an exclamation of pious gratitude to heaven, (Bull Dogge says it did not sound so to him), I seized it, and with the desperate strength of a dying man I renewed the battle, and eventually came off victorious and triumphant. Weary with slaughter, I fell exhausted on the bed, and slept till morning; Bull Dogge, who had been engaged in the same delightful occupation, appeared at the breakfast table with one eye black, and his face spotted like a he-tiger. We held a council of war, and resolved instantly to quit the premises of the Emerald Islander, who had agreed to "lodge and eat" us (the she-Cyclops), and who had so nearly fulfilled the latter clause by proxy.

Another search and another home. Here for a week things went on tolerably well; the steak was sometimes capable of mastication, the coffee wasn't *always* weak, nor the butter always strong; but one day there appeared at breakfast a dish of beef, (Bull Dogge asserts that it was the fossil remains of an omnibus horse)—it was not molested; at dinner it made its appearance again, still it was not disturbed; at tea fragments of it were visible, but it yet remained untouched; in the morning a tempting looking stew made its appearance, but, alas! it was only a weak invention of the enemy to conceal the ubiquitous beef; at dinner a meat-pie enshrined a portion of the aforesaid beef; it went away unharmed.

For a week, every day, at every meal, in every subtle form, in some ingenious disguise, still was forced upon our notice this omnipresent beef; it went through more changes than Harlequin in the Pantomime, and like that nimble individual came always out uninjured.

At the end of the second day Bull Dogge grumbled to himself; the third he spoke "out in meeting;" the fourth he growled audibly; the fifth he had an hour's swear to himself in his own room; the sixth, seventh, and eighth, he preserved a dignified silence; but his silence was ominous, on the ninth day we both left.

Our next landlady had a gigantic mouth, but her nose was a magnificent failure. We stayed with her a week, and left because she seemed to be possessed of the idea that one sausage was enough for two men. For a month longer we ran the gauntlet of all the model boarding-houses. We were entrapped by all kinds of alluring promises, and perpetually swindled without any regard to decency; we had a taste of Yankee, French, Dutch, and, I have mentioned it before, (ye gods!), *Irish;* and we lived four days in an establishment presided over by a red-eyed darkey, with a wife the color of a new saddle.

At last one day in an agony of despair I exclaimed, "Where, O where can humbugged humanity find a decent place to feed?" Echo answered, "In the eating-houses." We resolved to try it, and the result is glorious. We have achieved a victory, sir, an heroic, unexpected victory.

And now farewell, all scrawny landladies, ye snuffy beldames, with your wooden smiles; farewell, ye viviparous bedsteads, ye emaciated feather beds, and ye attenuated bolsters; a long good-bye to scant blankets and mattresses stuffed with shavings; farewell to hirsute butter and to ancient bread; good-bye (I say it with a tear,) ye immortal, everlasting beef; farewell to sloppy coffee and to azure milk (Damphool says, not yet); farewell ye antediluvian pies, and you lilliputian puddings; farewell you two-inch napkins, and ye *holy* table-cloths; farewell ye empty grates and rusty coal-scuttles; farewell ye cracked mirrors which make a man look like a drunken Satyr; farewell ye respectable chairs with dislocated limbs; farewell ye fractured teacups, ye broken forks, and knives with handsaw edges; farewell, in fact, all ye lodging houses, where you *can't* have a latch-key, and where you *can* tell when they get a new hired girl by the color of the hairs in the biscuit.

(I noticed this last remarkable fact a long time since.)

Give us joy, for we have found a place where things are done up right, where we can choose our own viands, where the beef is positively tender, where there are no little red ants in the sugar, where the potatoes are not waxy, and where, if anything goes wrong, we can inflate the waiter.

In fact, we are suited; if anything runs short, "John gets particular *fits*," and "nuthin' shorter;" where we can eat *when* we please, and call for *what* we please; where charges are moderate, and it is permitted to grumble at the waiter for nothing.

And here, in this Elysian spot, have Bull Dogge and I taken our daily bread (beans and butter included) for the past month, "without fear and without reproach."

As our poetical friend, Thomas Plus, has remarked,

> "Joy, joy, forever, our task is done,
> Our trials are past, and our Restaurant is *some*."

Damphool says my concluding quotation is not strictly correct, but what does he know about it?

# VIII.

## The Potency of Croton Water, or an aqueous quality hitherto unknown.

IT has been a cherished superstition of our ancestors that water as a beverage is innocuous; I myself was laboring under this infatuated delusion when I left the shades of private life, and the sweet retiracy of the swamps of Michigan, to become a denizen of the Island City.

Believing that my previous experience in the article justified me in drinking freely of the treacherous liquid, I did not hesitate on my arrival here to imbibe on various occasions as much of the undiluted Croton as my thirsty body seemed to need.

How I was deceived in the potency of the fluid a single night's experience will show; I am confident that on this particular occasion I was bewitched by the mischievous God of the stream called the Croton, and that, if I had given him any further opportunities to exercise his craft, my name would positively have appeared in the Police Reports some morning, and Doesticks would have been therein stigmatized as "*Drunk and Disorderly.*"

But the imputation would be slanderous,—I will lay before the public the events of a single night, and its verdict shall be a triumphant vindication of my character,—shall exculpate the Deity Bacchus (now resident in Ohio,) from the grave charge of leading me astray,—and lay the entire blame of the transaction upon the rascal River God.

Only once in my life have I been drunk. It was a youthful inebriation, caused by partaking too freely of cider made from apples with worms in them. At present I am sober. If, since my sojourn in this city, I have been intoxicated, then the time has arrived when any person who wishes to have a regular "drunk" need only apply to the nearest hydrant.

Heretofore I have supposed water to be a beverage innocent and harmless; but now—well; no matter—I will not anticipate. Listen while I relate a "plain, unvarnished tale."

I left my boarding-house in company with a friend, intending to witness the Shakspearian revival at Burton's—the "Midsummer Night's Dream." Before leaving the hotel, at his suggestion, we partook of a potable, known, I think, as punch—*whiskey punch.* I watched attentively the preparation of this agreeable beverage, and I am certain that there entered into its composition a certain amount of water—Croton water, as I have every reason to believe; and I am also sure that in that treacherous draught I imbibed the first instalment of that villanous liquid which produced the diabolical state of facts I am about to describe; and also that the second and third of those ingenious inventions (both of which we drank on the spot) were as guilty, in this respect, as their "illustrious predecessor!"

And I furthermore conscientiously state that *my* glass of brandy (one of a couple we ordered soon afterwards), and which, according to my invariable custom, should have been "*straight*," was also surreptitiously diluted with the same detestable fluid by the malicious bar-keeper, for I remember experiencing a slight confusion on going out, and mistaking a topsail schooner for the Broadway theatre.

We immediately entered another saloon to procure the wherewith to steady our nerves, when we partook of two gin cocktails and a brandy smash individually, and I state, according to the best of my knowledge and belief, that our principal ingredient in each and every one of these compounds was water—Croton water—culpably introduced therein by some evil-disposed persons without my knowledge or consent.

On leaving this saloon, I noticed that my friend, although a single man, had by some mysterious process of multiplication become two. I kept fast hold of both, and, after doubling, with a great deal of difficulty, a great number and variety of corners, we reached Burton's. Tickets being mysteriously procured, we entered, and eventually obtained seats. Finding, after prolonged trial, that it was impracticable to put my hat in my vest pocket, I placed it on the floor, and put both feet in it. The theatre generally seemed to be somewhat mixed up. The parquette, gallery, and dress circle were all one; and the stage was whirling round at a rate which must have been extremely inconvenient to the revolving actors.

At length, after a liberal allowance of overture, the curtain went up, and I was enabled, by the most unremitting attention, to concentrate the actors sufficiently to understand the performance. And many things which I hitherto deemed dramatically incorrect were presented to my wondering vision then and there.

"Hippolyta" was dressed in knee-breeches and brogans, and "Titania" did not, to me, present a very fairy-like appearance in a fireman's red shirt and a three-cocked hat. "Oberon" was not so objectionable (being a gentleman,) in a talma and plaid pantaloons, though even he might have blacked his boots and omitted the spurs. I fear I did not properly appreciate the rest of the fairies, who had their heads decorated with sunflowers and their hands full of onions.

At last the entertainment was concluded, and I remember consulting with my duplicated friend as to the feasibility of a return to Brooklyn, to our boarding-house. On our journey thither we witnessed many strange things about which I desire information.

In the first place, is it the custom, as a general thing, for the City Hall and Barnum's Museum to indulge in an animated contra-dance up and down Broadway in the middle of the night, accompanied in their fantastic movements, by the upper story of Stewart's and the Bible Society's building? For they certainly did on that eventful evening, and I feel called upon to enter my solemn protest against these nocturnal architectural saltatory exhibitions, as unworthy the dignity of the Empire City.

And I would, with all humility, suggest, that if the stony goddess of Justice, whose appropriate place is on the top of the City Hall, will desert her responsible post, she might choose a more becoming amusement than sitting cross-legged on the top of a Houston street stage, playing the jews-harp.

I am *now* convinced that Bowling-Green fountain is not *permanently* located on the top of Trinity Church cross; but that it *was* on that memorable night, my wondering eyes bore ample testimony.

I am sufficiently well acquainted with the city to know that the Astor House should be found on the corner of Barclay street, but I am ready to take my oath that on that particular occasion it plied as an opposition ferry-boat between Whitehall street and Hamilton avenue. The last thing I distinctly recollect is trying to pay the fare for three on this novel craft, with a single piece of money (which I *now* know to have been a Bungtown copper), and demanding two-and-sixpence change, which I didn't get.

In the morning I found myself in bed with my overcoat on, and afterwards discovered my boots under the pillow—my hat in the grate, with my pantaloons and hair-brush in it—my watch in the water-jug, and my latch-key in the bird-cage. I presume I had tried to write a letter to some one with my tooth-brush, as I found that article in my inkstand.

Now, if Croton water interferes with my susceptible system in this unaccountable manner, what shall I drink? I would resort to milk, but I fear our city edition of the lacteal contains sufficient of the aqueous enemy to again upset my too delicate nerves. I exclaim, like Cæsar, when he, too, was afflicted with superfluity of water, "Help me, Cassius, or I sink!"

What would be the effect of brandy and water without any water, and a little lemon?

## IX.

## Modern Witchcraft.

IT has been asserted, that no humbug can be invented which is so improbable that it will find no believers. No theory is too ridiculous, no folly too great to turn the stomach of the modern wonder-seeking Public; it opens its staring eyes, perhaps, a little wider than usual at some transcendent tomfoolery, but its sapient optics have as yet discerned nothing in all the superfluous deceptions and jugglery of the age, too hugely nonsensical to be swallowed without even a single qualm.

Hence, all the "pathies" and "isms" of medical Empiricism, all the newly discovered charlatanry of the legal trade, and even the latest form of religious quackery, that new device of bashful, half-grown, bastard Infidelity, denominated Spiritualism, which would be impious if it was not idiotic, have all received from the wise ones of the nineteenth century belief and credence.

For at this time of triumphant and successful humbug—when indiscriminate puffery is freely used to boost into notice all kinds of sham, deception, and deceit, which thereupon grow fat and thrive—when vermin exterminators, lucifer matches, and patent blacking employ such high-flown language in commendation of their merits, that inventions of real merit and importance must resort to the basest bombast to keep pace with the foolery of their neighbors—when solid merit which *would* succeed, must vie in euphuistic phrase with brainless emptiness which *will*—when, in Literature, inane collections of stolen wit, diluted humor, and feeble fiction are spawned in scores from weak-brained fops and aspiring women, inflated by unsparing puffery into a transient notoriety, and palmed upon the public as works of sterling merit—when even these Doestick Letters are purchased and perused, it may easily be imagined that no impudent humbug, if properly managed, will turn the stomach of the enlightened Yankee Nation.

It is not astonishing, that, in a sort of gross imitation of the clairvoyants and spirit-seers, other persons not quite so intellectual perhaps, but fully as reliable should also profess to hold converse with invisible beings.

The *fortune-tellers* of the city are these, and they certainly deserve praise for attempting to apply their pretended knowledge to some practical use, instead of dealing entirely with abstractions. In New York these people are numerous, and they pick up as many coppers in quite as honest a way as their fellows in the art of table-tipping notoriety.

Having read the advertisement of a Grand street fortune-teller, who advertised herself the "seventh daughter of a seventh daughter," a lineal descendant from some one of the Egyptian magicians who couldn't kill the frogs—I straightway resolved to pay her a visit.

Since that memorable day my destiny is no longer a mystery. I know it all. I know what kind of a woman I'm to marry, how many children we're to have, how many will die of measles, and how many will be choked with the croup, and can calculate to a quart how much castor oil I shall have to lay in for family consumption. I've had my fortune told by a witch.

The witches of modern time do not frequent graves and gibbets at midnight—they hold no nocturnal orgies with dancing skeletons and corpses, brought by the black art back to temporary life—they now-a-days take no pains to conceal their trade, but advertise it in the daily papers.

Their believers are not now the great men and wise women of the earth alone, but chamber-maids and servant girls who want love-powders to win some noble swain—or some verdant countryman anxious to recover the pilfered eelskin which contained his treasured pennies. They easily satisfy these gullible customers, by promising the first no end of rich, handsome princes, who are to appear some day and carry off their brides in four-horse coaches; and the latter by an extemporaneous description of the thief, and a wish that he may suffer pains in his head, heart, liver, and all other important parts of his body, until the property is restored.

Witchcraft is rife in our midst, and we do not hang or burn the hags and beldames who practise it, or stick them full of needles, or duck them in the horse-ponds, as in the good old days of Salem—more's the pity.

In this day of railroads and three-cent stages, they have no occasion to perform their journeys upon broomsticks; and in our city, where cream is only traditionary, they cannot bewitch their neighbors' churnings, or throw their dire enchantments over the incipient cheese—so the protective horse-shoe is of no avail.

They have robbed the trade of all its mystery and romance; we hear no more of mighty magian, with hoary beard and flowing robe, with magic wand and attendant spirits; no more "weird sisters," with talon fingers and sunken eyes; not even romantic wandering gipsies—but ugly women, with unwashed hands, who can't spell.

The calling has degenerated, and the necromantic trade has passed into the hands of unworthy successors, who would steal their living, if cheating wasn't easier. And the trade thrives, and the swindling practisers thereof flaunt in silks, while honest virtue staves off destitution by making "hickory" shirts at eight cents a-piece.

Went up town, found the house, rung the bell, and was shown into a shabby room by a stuttering girl, who informed me by instalments that her mistress would see me presently. Examined the furniture—rickety table, ditto chairs, bare floor with knot-holes in it, unctuous mirror, two hair trunks, a clothes basket, and a hat-box.

Enter mistress—minus youth, beauty, hair-pins and clean stockings.

She wore no flowing robe figured with cabalistic signs, she bore no sable wand of magic, but she was clad in a calico dress, and had a brass candlestick in her hand—she drew no mystic circle, she performed no inscrutable incantations, she spoke in no unknown tongue—but she put the candlestick on the rickety table, sat down in a cane-bottomed chair, and asked me what my name was, and what I wanted.

Told her I wanted to find out who I was going to marry, and wanted her to tell me a lucky number in the lottery, which should draw a prize big enough to support the family—also wanted a description of the man who stole my jack-knife, and a knowledge of the place where I could find the same.

Now she began to work—she did not consult the stars—she did not cast my horoscope—she did not even ask me where I was born, or what my father did for a living—she exhibited no strange paraphernalia of sorcery and conjuration—no obscure language, suggestive of a divination or enchantment, fell from her prophetic lips.

She only asked me if I had any moles on my person, and what I dreamed about last night—then plunging her hand through a slit in the side of her dress, she fished out from some unknown depth a pack of cards. Greasy were they, and well worn—the knave of spades had his legs torn off, the queen of diamonds had her face scratched with a thimble, two of the aces were stuck together with beeswax, and the king of clubs had evidently been used to skim flies out of the molasses.

After much shuffling of the royal and plebeian members of the pack, she got them fixed to her satisfaction, and I proceeded to draw therefrom nine cards, which she disposed in three symmetrical piles; then looked them over—bit her lip—stamped her foot; then told me that my knife had been stolen by a squint-eyed Irishman, who had disposed of it to his uncle for a dozen cotton night-caps, sixty cigars and thirty cents ready money, and that if I was anxious to reclaim it, I would find it at No. 1 Round the Corner.

Asked her if I was big enough to lick the Irishman, at which she waxed indignant, and for a moment I half feared she would turn me into some horrible monster; that, like Circe of old, she would exercise her magic power, and qualify me to play a star engagement at the Metropolitan Theatre by transforming me into an elephant, a she-wolf, or a Bengal tiger.

But, as my mouth didn't get any larger, my toe nails grow any longer, or my fingers change to claws; as I felt no growing appetite for blood, and my nose didn't elongate into a trunk, I soon recovered my equanimity.

Then she went on to say that No. 67 would draw me a prize in the lottery, and that I could get it of "Sam"—that I would marry a red-haired woman, who would die and leave me with a nursing baby—that I would then be "jilted" by a widow, and finally wed a lady whose description corresponds exactly with my present washer-woman; our family is to increase to seventeen; my second son is to be President, and my eldest daughter is to run away with the Czar of all the Russias. She wasn't exactly positive about the manner of my death, but from the looks of the jack of clubs, she "judged I should break my neck coming home from a clam-bake."

Gave her a dollar, and left. A month has passed—67 seems a promising number—hav'n't got my knife yet, but live in hope—have seen my future wife, hav'n't yet proposed, but have reason to suppose she would not object.

She was in Catharine street, and had a basket on her head full of shrimps.

City Target Excursion.

## X.

# City Target Excursion.

IN this City, which, even in cholera seasons, is most heroically nasty, when the filth in Broadway gets so deep as to stop the stages and throw the cars off the track, men are sent round by the City to expend an infinity of labor in hoeing it into symmetrical heaps, like miniatnre fortifications. In fact, if plenitude of mud could avail to protect a town from invading foes, New York might bid the world defiance, for all the allied powers of all the earth could no more reduce our (in that case) impregnable City, than the late chivalrous Lord Forth could take Sebastopol, by lying flat on his back, and calling for his ma to come and take him home. As the City authorities content themselves with *erecting* these picturesque monuments, and do not trouble themselves to remove the same, but leave them to adorn the landscape, of course the first rain metamorphoses the fragrant mass from an embryo mountain to a diminutive lake, almost disgusting enough to make a street contractor sick. No lady attempts the perilous navigation of our streets, unless she has been a couple of seasons at Newport or Rockaway, and learned to swim like a mermaid. And any man who would black his boots in the morning, would be taken to the Lunatic Asylum before night. A search for a dry crossing would be a hopeless pilgrimage, and he who would find a get-over-able-without-getting-your-shoes-full-of-mud street in this metropolis, would wear his life out in a fruitless exploration, and be prematurely planted in Greenwood, with his object unattained. In ordinary times the ladies sweep the sidewalks tolerably clean with their trailing skirts, but now they seem to have thrown up their contract. Coming down town the other day in a stage, our reckless driver tried the depth of one of the above-mentioned municipal lakes—the wheels stuck fast—the vehicle settled into the hopeless depth—one scream from the ladies—one unanimous curse from the men—one frantic, furious, ineffectual struggle of the horses, and in another instant we were floating a hopeless wreck. Every one for himself. I saw one of the ladies dragged safely out by the hair—

men eventually reached the land in safety, but I rejoiced to see a malignant baby, (which during our journey had screamed and kicked one half the time, and the other half persisted in calling me "Daddy," and soiling my shirt-front with its sticky fingers,) go to the bottom amid a universal chorus of thanksgiving from the company. Got ashore myself, with my coat spoiled, my hat minus, my boots full of water, and my whole person "dripping from the recent flood," like a he-Venus rising from an odoriferous ocean.

As a consequence of my involuntary bath, I have since been afflicted with a severe toothache, pleading which comfortable and soothing ail, I obtained leave of absence for a day from the popular establishment where I have the honor to sell peanuts and pop-corn to the confiding public, and I resolved to employ the unusual holiday in attending one of the peculiar institutions of grown-up New York, denominated a "TARGET SHOOT."

From the incongruous population of the village aforesaid, target companies spring up with the rapidity and profusion of mushrooms in an old pasture. In all other cities they are exotics, and never have a vigorous and healthy existence—here only are they indigenous, and on Manhattan Island do they flourish in native luxuriance.

The materials are varied—the ingredients sometimes curious—a company being sometimes composed entirely of journeymen tailors, blacksmiths' apprentices, master carpenters, clerks, porters, coalheavers, stagedrivers, candy-peddlers, pop-corn men, or those persevering individuals who roast perpetual chestnuts on the sidewalk in tin pans—fire companies, express companies, policemen, gangs of men from all kinds of mammoth shops—for wherever thirty or forty individuals work in the same house, they form themselves into a military company, and once or twice every year go to Hoboken and shoot for whiskey and other prizes.

When they want to make a full turn-out, the places of any missing members are filled by extemporaneous volunteers. It was in this capacity that I proposed to go. In these companies there are always more officers than men, more epaulettes than muskets—always a big band of music, and two darkies to carry the target. As to their marching, no two ever step together, and they always put a tall man by the side of a short one, so as to have the average length of steps come right. They go forth in the morning in high spirits, and return at night surly, dusty, discontented, dilapidated, and drunk. As the target is always carried in triumph through the streets, and afterward exhibited in the drill-room, the darkey invariably carries an auger with him, with which explosive weapon all the best shots are made. Every member has a whiskey-bottle in his cartridge-box, or a brandy-flask in his knapsack.

As a general thing, they turn their toes in, and are bandy-legged—they carry their guns over their shoulders at all conceivable angles, and so little do they know about fire-arms, that probably, if called to load their muskets in a hurry, two out of three would put their cartridges in their breeches pockets, and stick their percussion caps on the ends of their ramrods.

When they fire salute, and mean to all shoot together, the report is so near simultaneous that a stranger would think they were firing minute guns. They always select for judges of the shooting, the men who will give the most whiskey, and make the shortest speeches.

As these excursions come off just before election, the candidates for office generally pay for the prizes, and bear the expenses of a reporter for the press to puff the company. The judges carry out the re wards in the morning tied up in brown paper, and the soldiers wear them back at night, around their necks. Six or eight men, called pioneers, march in front, with muffs on their heads, leather aprons tied around their waists, and theoretical axes in their hands, which could never, by any possibility, be made to cut anything. The officers walk between the platoons, flourishing their dandy swords—their attention being pretty equally divided between keeping the men in the line, keeping the little boys out of the line, keeping their unaccustomed white cotton gloves on, and trying to keep step with the music. In single file the men march like a flock of geese on their winding way to the mill-pond, and six or eight abreast, they go with the regularity of a crowd of school-boys, effecting a masterly but hurried retreat from somebody's melon-patch. In order to make them form a straight line, it is necessary to back them up against a brick block, or make them stand between the tracks of a railroad.

Such was the company of which I became a member for a brief eventful time. Its cognomen was "The Lager-Bier American Volunteers, and Native Empire City Shillelagh Guards," being composed of Irish, Dutch, Spaniards, and Sandwich Islanders —the only Americans in the company being the colored target-bearers, and the undersigned.

Convened in the drill-room at 8 A. M. As I was a new member, and had borrowed my uniform, I had some difficulty in putting it on—buckled my crossbelt round my neck, got my cap on wrong side before, stuck my bayonet through my coat-tail—put my cartridge-box between my shoulders, and my priming-wire where my "pompon" should have been.

Ready at length to start—crossed the ferry—disembarked—proceeded to the ground and prepared to drill.

The captain finding it impossible to get into a straight line in the usual manner, at length ingeniously overcame this geometrical difficulty by ranging us against a board fence—he then proceeded to put us through the exercise: "Shoulder arms!" Got my gun on the wrong shoulder. "Order arms!" Brought it down on the toes of my neighbor. "Shoulder arms!" again. Got it on the right shoulder this time, but in so doing knocked off the cap of the man next to me, &c. Got through the rest of the drill without any serious mishap, except that in attempting to charge my piece, I bit off the wrong end of the cartridge, and swallowed the ball—spilled the powder on the ground, and loaded the musket with the paper only.

Now came the shooting. Nigger set the target at twenty paces—four volleys and not a ball in it—moved it up to fifteen—no better luck—moved it again, one ball put in it this time by a clumsy Dutchman, who shut his eyes when he fired, and hit by mistake. Finding that shooting was no use, captain adopted the usual plan—set the target at ten paces, blindfolded the men, and each one charged on it with the auger; where the point happened to hit, he bored a hole, and the one nearest the bull's eye took the prize. I could see a little through a hole in the cloth—consequence: hit the centre and took the first prize, (a plated cake-basket with a pewter handle, bought for silver by the sagacious Committee).

As the brandy had circulated pretty freely, some of the shots were rather wild—several missed the target entirely and knocked their heads against the trees; one bored a deep hole in a sand bank, and the first lieutenant was put under arrest for attempting to tap the captain.

The man who took the second prize did not come

so near the mark by an inch and a half as another man, but he had a pretty sister whom one of the judges was in love with, so he took "the spoons." Ready to go home—Muggins, one of the judges, missing. After a long search found him wrapped up in the colors, fast asleep with his head in a hog-trough—stirred him up with a musket, when he called me "Mrs. Muggins," and swore at me for pulling all the sheet over to my side.

Marched home in as good order as circumstances would allow—the darkey bearing in proud triumph the perforated target, which had so many hits near the centre, as to excite the admiration of the deluded public, which, as a general rule, in such cases, can't tell a bullet mark from an auger-hole.

## XI.

### A new Patent Medicine Operation.

AS I too desire to have a mansion on the Fifth Avenue, like the Medical Worthy of Sarsaparilla memory, and wished like him to be able to build a patent medicine palace, with a private chapel under the back-stairs, and a conservatory down-cellar, I cast about me for some means whereby the requisite cash might be reputably accumulated.

I feared that the Panacea and Cure-Everything trick had been played too often, but I determined to make one big try, and I think that at last my fortune is made.

Congratulate me—I am immortalized, and I've done it myself. My name will be handed down to posterity as that of a universal benefactor. The hand which hereafter writes upon the record of Fame, the names of Ayer, Sands, Townsend, Moffat, Morrison, and Brandreth, must also inscribe, side by side with these distinguished appellations, the no less brilliant cognomen of the undying Doesticks.

Emulous of the deathly notoriety which has been acquired by the medicinal worthies just mentioned, *I* also resolved to achieve a name and a fortune in the same reputable and honest manner.

Bought a gallon of tar, a cake of beeswax, and a firkin of lard, and in twenty-one hours I presented to the world the first batch of "*Doesticks' Patent, Self-Acting, Four-Horse Power Balsam,*" designed to cure all diseases of mind, body, or estate, to give strength to the weak, money to the poor, bread and butter to the hungry, boots to the barefoot, decency to blackguards, and common sense to the Know-Nothings. It acts physically, morally, mentally, psychologically, physiologically, and geologically, and it is intended to make our sublunary sphere a blissful paradise, to which Heaven itself shall be but a side-show.

I have not yet brought it to absolute perfection, but even now it acts with immense force, as you will perceive by the accompanying testimonials and records of my own individual experience. You will observe that I have not resorted to the usual manner of preparing certificates: which is, to be certain that all those intended for Eastern circulation shall seem to come from some formerly unheard-of place in the West, while those sent to the West shall be dated at some place forty miles east of sun-rise. But I send to *you*, as representing the western country, a certificate from an Oregon farmer.

"DEAR SIR: The land composing my farm has hitherto been so poor that a Scotchman couldn't get his living off it; and so stony that we had to slice our potatoes and plant them edgeways; but, hearing of your balsam, I put some on the corner of a ten-acre lot, surrounded by a rail-fence, and in the morning I found the rocks had entirely disappeared—a neat stone wall encircled the field, and the rails were split into ovenwood and piled up symmetrically in my back yard.

Put half an ounce into the middle of a huckleberry swamp—in two days it was cleared off, planted with corn and pumpkins, and ad a row of peach trees in full bloom through the middle.

As an evidence of its tremendous strength, I would state that it drew a striking likeness of my eldest daughter—drew my youngest boy out of the mill-pond—drew a blister all over his stomach—drew a load of potatoes four miles to market, and eventually drew a prize of ninety-seven dollars in the State Lottery.

And the effect upon the inhabitants hereabout has been so wonderful, that they have opened their eyes to the good of the country, and are determined to vote for a Governor who is opposed to frosts in the middle of June, and who will make a positive law against freshets, hail-storms, and the seventeen-year locusts."

There, isn't that *some?*

But I give one more from a member of the senior class in a western college, who, although misguided, neglected, and ignorant, is, undoubtedly, as honest and sincere as his Prussianized education will admit of.

I have corrected the orthography, and revised some grammatical inaccuracies; but, besides attending to these trifles, inserting marks of punctuation, and putting the capitals in the right places, I assure you I have made no alteration.

"Sall Harbor, June 31, 1854.

"My Dear Doctor. [You know I attended medical lectures half a winter, and once assisted in getting a crooked needle out of a baby's leg; so I understand perfectly well the theory and practice of medicine, and the *Doctor* is perfectly legitimate under the Prussian system.] By the incessant study required in this establishment, I had become worn down so thin that I was obliged to put on an overcoat to cast a shadow—but accidentally hearing of your Balsam, I obtained a quantity, and, in obedience to the Homœopathic principles of this Institution, took an *infinitesimal* dose only; in four days I measured one hundred and eighty-two inches round the waist; could chop eleven cords of hickory wood in two hours and a half; and, on a bet, carried a yoke of oxen two miles and a quarter in my left hand, my right being tied behind me, and if any one doubts the fact, the oxen are still to be seen.

"About two weeks after this, I had the pleasure of participating in a gunpowder explosion, on which occasion my arms and legs were scattered over the village, and my mangled remains pretty equally distributed throughout the entire county.

Under these circumstances my life was despaired of, and my classmates had bought a pine coffin, and borrowed whole shirts to attend the funeral in; when the invincible power of your four horse-power balsam (which I happened to have in my vest pocket) suddenly brought together the scattered pieces of my body—collected my limbs from the rural districts—put new life into my shattered frame, and I was restored, uninjured to my friends, with a new set of double teeth.

I have preserved the label which enveloped the bottle, and have sewed it into the seat of my pantaloons, and I now bid grim death defiance, for I feel that I am henceforth unkillable, and in fact I am even now generally designated the '*Great Western Achilles.*'

Yours entirely SKI HY."

I feel that after this, I need give you no more reports of third persons, but will detail some of my own personal experience of the article.

I caused some to be applied to the Washtenaw Bank after its failure, and while the Balsam lasted the Bank redeemed its notes with specie.

The cork of one of the bottles dropped upon the head of a childless widow, and in six weeks she had a young and blooming husband.

Administered some to a hack-driver in a glass of gin and sugar, and that day he swindled but seven people, and only gave two of them bad money in change.

Gave a few drops gratis to a poor woman who was earning a precarious subsistence by making calico shirts with a one-eyed needle, and the next day she was discovered to be heir to a large fortune.

Gave some to an up-town actor, and that night he said " damned" only twenty-one times.

One of the daily papers got the next dose, and in the next edition but one there were but four editorial falsehoods, seven indecent advertisements, and two columns and a half of home-made " Foreign Correspondence."

Caused fifteen drops to be given to the low comedian of a Broadway Theatre, and that night he was positively dressed more like a man than a monkey, actually spoke some lines of the author, made only three inane attempts at puerile witticisms—only twice went out of his way to introduce some grossly indelicate line into his part, and for a wonder, lost so much of his self-conceit that for a full half-hour he did not believe himself the greatest comedian in the world.

Gave some to a news-boy, and he manufactured but three fires, a couple of murders, and one horrible rail-road accident, in the next thirty minutes.

Put some on the outside of the Crystal Palace and the same day the stock went from 22 up to 44.

Our whole Empire City is entirely changed by the miraculous power of "Doesticks' Patent Self-Acting Four Horse Power Balsam." The gas is lighted on the dark nights, instead of on the moonlight evenings—there are no more highway robberies in the streets, or, if there are, the offenders, when arrested, are instantly discharged by the police magistrate. No more building materials on the sidewalks; no more midnight murders; no more Sunday rows; no more dirty streets; no more duels in Hoboken, and no more lies in the newspapers.

Broadway is swept and garnished: the M. P.'s are civil, and the boys don't steal any more dogs. In fact, so well content are we now with our City, that we feel, as the Hibernian poet so beautifully says:

> "O, if there be an Elysium on earth,
> It is this—it is this."

Orders for my Balsam, *accompanied by the money*, will be immediately attended to; otherwise not, for my partner and I have resolved to sell for cash only feeling as did Dr. Young, who appropriately and feelingly remarks—

"We take no notes on Time."

Bull Dogge says I have piled it up too strong, and that no one will believe what he calls "that humbug about the newspapers, and the preposterous nonsense concerning the Broadway Actor." I am aware that in these instances my medicine has performed a modern miracle, but the facts remain "no less true than strange."

If I fail to accumulate a "pile" in this speculation, I shall start a Know-Nothing Newspaper, run it a month, and then fail and swindle the subscribers; get an overgrown woman or a whiskered lady, and exhibit her for twenty-five cents a head, or get up a Grand Gift Enterprise, with $20,000 prizes.

## XII.

### Running with the "Masheen."

SINCE the "*Grate old Squwirt*" made to go by steam, and imported from Cincinnati to put to the blush Metropolitan Redshirtdom, and which couldn't raise steam enough to throw water to the top of the City Hall, has proved such a signal failure, the good old-fashioned "fire-annihilators" (not Barnum's) have been more popular than ever.

The "boys" say they will take the oldest and most primitive engine in the city, man it with fourteen small-sized news-boys on a side, and, with this apparatus, will throw more water, throw it higher farther, and to more purpose than any or all the clumsy steam humbugs yet invented in Porkopolis.

Ninety-seven's boys say they can run to a fire, get their water on, extinguish the conflagration, "take-up," get home, bunk in, and snooze half an hour before the "Squwirt" could get her kindling-wood ready.

Doesticks Running with the "Masheen."

Now I am not known by the cognomen of "Mose," nor do I answer to the name of "Syskey"—neither as a general thing do I promenade the middle of Broadway with my pantaloons tucked into my boots. Still, by way of a new excitement, I lately joined the Fire Department, and connected myself with the company of Engine 97.

Bought my uniform, treated the company, took up my quarters in the bunkroom, where I slept by night in a bed occupied in the day-time by a big yellow dog. First night, went to bed with my boots on, ready for an alarm. At last it came—seized the rope with the rest of the boys; started on a run; tugged and toiled till we got her into the 11th district, four miles and a half from home; found the alarm hac been caused by a barrel of shavings, and the conflagration had extinguished itself; had to drag her clear back; tired most to death; it wasn't funny at all.

Turned in; half an hour, new alarm; started again—hose 80 laid in the same alley, got our apparatus jammed on the corner; fight; 97 victorious; got our machine out, and carried off the forewheel of 80's carriage on our tongue; reached the fire; big nigger standing on the hydrant; elected myself appraiser and auctioneer; knocked him down without any bidder; took water; got our stream on the fire; fun; worked till my arms ached; let go to rest; foreman hit me over the head with a trumpet, and told me to go ahead; children in the garret; horrible situation; gallant fireman made a rush up the ladder; battled his way through the smoke—re-appeared with a child in each arm, and his pocket full of teaspoons.

Old gentleman from the country; much excited; wanted to help, but didn't exactly know how; he rushed into a fourth-story bedroom; threw the mirror out of the window; frantically endeavored to hurl the dressing-table after it; seized the coal-scuttle; hurriedly put in the poker, bootjack, and a pair of worn out slippers, carried them down stairs, and deposited them in a place of safety four blocks away; came back on a run, into the parlor; took up the door-mat, wrapped up an empty decanter in it, and transported it safely into the barn of the nearest neighbor; he kept at work; by dint of heroic exertions, he at various times deposited, by piece, the entire kitchen cooking-stove in the next street, uninjured; and at last, after knocking the piano to pieces with an axe, in order to save the lock, and filling his pocket with the sofa castors, he was seen to make his final exit from the back-yard, with a length of stovepipe in each hand, the toasting fork tucked behind his ear, and two dozen muffin rings in his hat, which was surmounted by a large-sized frying-pan.

During the next week there were several alarms—fire in a big block full of paupers—first man in the building; carried down stairs in my arms two helpless undressed children, thereby saving their valuable lives; on giving them to their mother, she, amid a whirlwind of thanks, imparted the gratifying intelligence that one was afflicted with the measles, and the other had the Michigan itch.

Another fire; foreman took the lead, and ran down the street, yelling like an independent devil, with a tin trumpet. Company made a grand stampede, and followed in the rear, dragging old 97 in a spasmodic gallop. Found the fire in a boarding school; dashed up a ladder; tumbled through a window; entered a bed-room; smoke so thick I couldn't see; caught up in my arms a feminine specimen in a long night-gown; got back to the window; tried to go down; ladder broke under me; stuck adhesively to the young lady; and, after unexampled exertions, deposited her safely in the next house, where I discovered that I had rescued from the devouring element the only child of *the black cook!*

Fire in a storehouse—went on the roof; explosion; found myself in somebody's cellar, with one leg in a soap barrel, and my hair full of fractured hen's eggs; discovered that I had been blown over a church, and had the weathercock still remaining in the rear of my demolished pantaloons.

Fire in a liquor-store—hose burst; brandy "lying round loose;" gin "convaynient," and old Monongahela absolutely begging to be protected from further dilution; Croton water too much for my delicate constitution; carried home on a shutter.

Fire in a church—Catholic—little marble images all round the room in niches; wall began to totter; statues began to fall; St. Andrew knocked my fire hat over my eyes; St. Peter threw his whole weight on my big toe; St. Jerome hit me a clip over the head, which laid me sprawling, when a picture of the Holy Family fell and covered me up like a bed quilt.

Fire in a big clothing store—next day our foreman sported a new silk velvet vest, seven of the men exhibited twelve dollar doeskin pants, and the black boy who sweeps out the bunk room, and scours the engine, had a new hat, and a flaming red cravat, presented, as I heard, by the proprietor of the stock of goods, as an evidence of his appreciation of their endeavors to save his property.

*I* didn't get any new breeches; on the contrary, lost my new overcoat, and got damaged myself. Something like this—fire out, order came, "take up, 97;" took off the hose; turned her round; got the boys together, and started for home; corner of the street hook and ladder 100 (Dutch), engine 73 (Irish), hose 88 (Yankee), and our own company, came in contact; machines got jammed; polyglot swearing by the strength of the companies; got all mixed up; fight; one of 88's men hit foreman of hook and ladder 100 over the head with a spanner; extemporaneous and impartial distribution of brickbats; 97's engineer clipped one of 73's men with a trumpet; 73 retaliated with a paving stone; men of all the companies went in; resolved to "go in" myself; went in; went out again as fast as I could, with a black eye, three teeth (indigestible, I have reason to believe) in my stomach, intermingled with my supper, my red shirt in carpet rags, and my knuckles skinned, as if they had been pawned to a Chatham street Jew.

Got on a hydrant, and watched the fun; 88's boys whipped everything; 73's best man was doubled up like a jack-knife, by a dig in the place where Jonah was; four of 97's fellows were lying under the machine, with their eyes in mourning; hook and ladder took home two-thirds of their company on the truck, and the last I saw of their foreman he was lying in the middle of the street, with his trumpet smashed flat, his boots under his head, his pockets inside out, a brick in his mouth, a hundred and twenty-five feet of hose on the back of his neck, and the hind wheels of 20's engine resting on his left leg.

Four policemen, on the opposite corner, saw the whole row. On the first indication of a fight, they pulled their hats down over their eyes, covered up their stars, and slunk down the nearest alley. Got home, resigned my commission, made my will, left the company my red shirt and fire cap. Seen enough of fire service; don't regret my experience, but do grieve for my lost teeth and my new over coat.

P. S.—Have just met the foreman of 73—he had

on my late lamented overcoat; ain't big enough to lick him—magnanimously concluded to let him alone.

## XIII.

### Street Preaching—A Zealous Trio, and a Religious Controversy.

DURING the first part of my sojourn in the metropolis I made the acquaintance of a portly personage from the "Providence Plantations," who invited me to visit his home, and take a look at little "Rhody." As I had been hustled round pretty constantly for several weeks, I had become fairly tired of New York, although it is a town of considerable consequence. Wanted to see the world; so started for the seven-by-nine State of Rhode Island. In the course of a thorough exploration of that delightful though diminutive state, which occupied me about five hours, I discovered that they shingle the houses all over outside and in, and put the windows in the roof; they make their rail fences out of cobble stones; the ducks roost on the fence, and hatch their young ones in the tops of the cherry trees; the men look so much alike, their wives often kiss the wrong individual, (Damphool says it's a way women have the world over).

Went to the city of Providence, where all the men make jewelry, and all the women believe in spirit rappings; where they've got a bridge wider than it is long, and Macadamized on both sides; where all the plaster busts of great men have grey wigs on; where they light the gas in the middle of the afternoon; where they drive five horses tandem; where the apples grow as big as washtubs, and the oysters obtain the enormous size of three-cent pieces.

Went into the woods after chestnuts; couldn't find any, but discovered a magnificent tree in the distance—rejoiced exceedingly thereat—started for it—three quarters of a mile away; went ahead over stones, ditches, fences, snakes, briers, and stone walls, until at last I reached it, and found it was an elm, no chestnuts on it—got very mad; walked round the state a couple of times, and took the first train for home.

Glad to see the old place again, and also pleased to perceive that something of unusual importance seemed to occupy the attention of the usually-hard-at-work-but-on-Sunday-loafing-about-the-streets-waiting-for-a-fire-or-a-row-to-turn-up population of the city.

Saw a big crowd in the Park—inquired about it, and was told the usual Street Screeching was going on—wanted to see the fun—got a good place on a fat Irishman's toes.

Enter Gabriel—tin horn—hole in his pantaloons—(Bull Dogge says that if Angels have wings they are also provided with tails—hence this last item); thought it extremely probable. Gabriel mounted one end of the City Hall steps, and after a preliminary overture on his horn, and a slight skirmish among the faithful, resulting in four black eyes, a damaged nose, and a broken leg, the religious services commenced—(Damphool was entirely carried away by his sympathies for this last martyr, but soon discovered that the fractured member was "purely vegetable," as the patent medicine men say, and the injury was speedily repaired by means of a few shingle nails and a piece of clapboard).

Gabriel went in to win, but, spite of the sanctity of his name and the holiness of his aforesaid breeches, he was not permitted a clear field.

A female, with bosom undressed in the latest fashion; petticoats (Damphool says skirticoats) not immaculate; stockings, through the texture of which her delicate ancles were plainly visible to the naked eye; whose hair resembled molasses candy; with a nose symmetrical as an overgrown sweet potatoe, and in hue not unlike the martyred lobster; and whose teeth reminded me forcibly of the "crags and peaks" mentioned by the man in the play, took up her station on the other end of the steps.

She, like Gabe, went in for giving the church of Rome "Jesse," but otherwise did not agree with him. Did not seem willing to go to heaven by his conveyance, but claimed to have discovered some kind of a northwest passage—some exclusive path "cross lots;" and she advocated her right of way with all her woman's power of tongue—in fact, they agreed only tolerably—"Arcades ambo"—both celestials, but of a different breed—(B. D. says that some time since they joined issue on the devil's head, one asserting that he has horns, and the other maintaining that his brimstone friend is a muley)—but they both pitched into the Pope, abused all foreigners, denounced the church of Rome, walked into the affections of the Catholics generally—talked learnedly of priests, inquisitions, dungeons, thumbscrews, martyrs, convents, nunneries, and other luxuries, as being the only legitimate offspring of the mother of abominations, the scarlet woman; and, in fact, seemed to be having the field entirely to themselves, when lo! a change came o'er the spirit of the gospel show, for in the midst of the crowd suddenly appeared a third combatant—his classic dress and intellectual face gave unmistakable evidence that he was from the "gim of the ocean." With the dignified and majestic bearing peculiar to his countrymen, he slowly mounted the steps, and took a position directly between the two, and in a voice strongly tinctured with the "sweet brogue," announced himself as a champion of that much slandered gentleman, the Pope of Rome.

At this astounding impudence, the woman for a single instant held her peace. Gabe was so taken aback that he seemed about to collapse, but rallied, played an "ad libitum" interlude on the tin horn, and all hands "pitched in."

Gabriel commenced the onset by asserting that the Pope is not strictly a bachelor, but has seven white wives in his parlor, thirteen ditto bound in law calf in the library, a hundred and forty-one golden-haired damsels in his private apartments, and a perfect harem of jetty beauties in the coal-hole.

Petticoats followed, by saying that he breakfasts on Protestant babies; drinks whiskey punch out of a Protestant clergyman's skull; has an abducted Protestant virgin to black his boots; fifty-seven Protestant widows to dig his potatoes and hoe corn; and that he rolls ten-pins every afternoon with the heads of Protestant orphan children.

Irishman indignantly denied all—said the country is going to the old Knick, and some fine morning we shall wake up, and find that the Pope, unable longer to endure our perverseness, has sunk us all forty miles deeper than ancient Sodom; said that his Holiness can send us all to perdition by one wink of his left eye; that he is the head of the Church on Earth; has all power to save or otherwise; could get us all out of Purgatory, and send us all "kitin into Heaven," by wagging his little finger; that he could, like a Joshua No. 2, make the sun and moon stand still; make the planets dance an astronomical rigadoon; cause the hills and mountains to execute a mighty geological jig, while old ocean should beat the time against the blue vault of Heaven and applauding Angels encore the huge saltations.

Gabe said he didn't believe the yarn. Petticoats remarked something about the Star Spangled Banner being always right side up.

Irishman proceeded to describe the future home of the happy in another world, as a place where there shall be plenty of potatoes, no end of shillelahs, oceans of genuine whiskey; and where no Know-Nothing Yankee shall be allowed to come and kick up a plug muss.

At the word Know-Nothing, there was a great sensation. Symptoms of a free fight rapidly developed into an uncivil war. Petticoats got mixed up with the crowd, and presently emerged rather the worse for wear, barefooted, bareheaded, hair down, nose injured by collision, eye in mourning, mouth bloody, and her whole appearance reminding me of "a goose or goslin—stuffed." (I forgot who penned this apposite quotation, and asked Bull Dogge, who, being excited by the fray, angrily asserted that it is by "Nero or some other old fogy" —is it?)

Irishman was taken away by seven policemen, on

his national carriage, a wheelbarrow. Gabriel came out unhurt, save that his elegant features were somewhat marred by the finger nails of Petticoats. Perceiving that the fun was over, I turned to go, leaving the self-elected Angel Gabriel, straddle of a hydrant, edifying the passers-by, by alternately sounding notes of victory upon his horn, and crowing like an overgrown Shanghae.

## XIV.

### Disappointed Love.

ALTHOUGH in the course of my western peregrinations I had frequently met with attractive-looking damsels, there was always some blemish on their personal beauty, which though perhaps slight in many cases, made their charms fall short of that exalted standard desirable in the fairer part of mankind. Being unusually fastidious in my taste it is not to be wondered at, that previous to last Wednesday night, I had never been in love.

Save an occasional fit of cholera-morbus, I had never experienced anything even remotely approaching the tender passion. But on the evening of the eventful Wednesday, Sandie Goatie invited me to go with him and see his sister.

Now my friend Sandie is not a scholarly person, and has never received that questionable blessing, a college educat'on. He always says "cod-fish" instead of "bonâ fide," and calls "tempus fugit" "pork and beans;" the only "Jupiter" he knows is a sable gentleman, and his only idea of "Venus," is a colored washerwoman, who in early life got up his hebdomadal linen.

But his sister is eminently classic; she stoops fashionably, with the "Grecian bend"—has a Roman nose, and her name is Calanthe Maria.

I went to see that sister—I *saw* that sister—I surrendered.

That seraphic sister—to attempt a description of her beauty, would be insanity itself. I will only mention her hair, and when I have said that this was sublime and divine, I wish it distinctly understood that I use these feeble terms, because the poverty of our language does not afford adjectives of adequate force.

The instant I saw her, my presence of mind deserted me. I felt bashful—I was conscious that I looked like a fool in the face, and my apparel, (on which I had prided myself), seemed as unworthy to be seen in her presence, as if it had been bought second-hand in Chatham street. Beneath the glance of her brilliant eyes, my feet seemed to grow too short, and my legs too long—my coat too big, and my co lar limpsy, and I discovered a grease spot on my vest. Never had I been so shamefaced in the feminine presence before, and my bashfulness only temporarily deserted me, when, after much tribulation, I achieved a seat on a clumsy looking foot-stool, which I understood was called an "Ottoman." Whether or not it had any connection with Turks, turkeys, and Thanksgiving, I failed to discover.

Left alone a short time, I had leisure to recover myself, and to note the individual charms of my fair enslaver. A partial inventory of her visible apparel is ineffaceably stamped upon my mind.

A silk dress, of a pattern which seemed to have been designed for a gigantic checker-board, made with a train to do scavenger duty, and short sleeves, with lace curtains underneath—her neck and shoulders hidden from view by a thin veil of transparent lace, of a pattern designedly made to attract attention—but particulars are omitted.

Suffice it to say, that she was dressed as the prevailing fashion seems to demand.

I essayed to speak to her, but my timidity returned upon me with double force. Mustered courage at length and asked her to sing, and stepped on her toes while turning over her music—praised everything in the wrong place—when she sung a false note, I exclaimed ' delicious." She made a two-handed discord, which I pronounced "enchanting," and when at last, from excess of agitation, she broke flat down, I enthusiastically declared that I was "never more delighted in the whole course of my life."

Asked her to play a waltz, and handed her a choir-book—opened at "Corinth" and "Silver street"—found I was wrong, and turned over the leaf to "Sinners turn, why will ye die?"—discovered that all was not right yet, and then requested her to play some sacred music, and in my anxiety to get the right notes this time, placed before her the "Jenny Lind Polka," which she at once began to play—I attempting to sing the words of "Old Hundred," which didn't seem to jibe.

We tried to dance, but my confusion still continued. I "chassezéd" myself across a table, and into a music rack—"promenaded" my partner over the stove—"balanced" her into a side-board, and eventually attempted to seat her in a mirror, where I saw a sofa.

Then I essayed conversation, and I am confident I talked the most absurd nonsense for the rest of my call—distinctly remember speaking of Noah Webster's beautiful play of "Evangeline"—eulogising Shakspeare's "Robinson Crusoe"—Thackeray's generalship at Waterloo—attempting to explain the difficulties which attended Henry Ward Beecher's attempts to get his Opera of "Bohemian Girl" before the public—telling who had the blackest eye when President Pierce and Joan of Arc fought their celebrated prize fight in the Crystal Palace in New York in 1793—and at last, breaking down in trying to explain why Admiral Elihu Burritt, and his right hand man Xerxes the Great, did not succeed in taking Sebastopol in a month, according to contract.

When I bid her "good night," she took my hand and set me crazy by the touch of her fairy, taper fingers.

I dreamed all night about Calanthe—got up in the morning, called the waiter "Calanthe," and said "my darling" to him as he handed me my coffee—gave my tailor an order for a new coat and two pairs of pantaloons, and told him to charge them to "Calanthe"—got a box of cigars and a demijohn of Scotch whiskey, and signed the drayman's receipt "Calanthe"—all the signs read "Calanthe"—every street was "Calanthe" street—all the stages belonged to the "Calanthe" line, and were going to "Calanthe" ferry—the ship "Calanthe" had arrived, the steamboat "Calanthe" had burst her boiler, and the brig "Calanthe" been seen bottom upward with her rudder gone. I saw, heard, read, dreamed, thought, and talked nothing but "Calanthe," and cannibal that I am, I verily believe I ate nothing but "Calanthe" for a month.

The day after I saw her first I felt so exceedingly amiable that I bought something of every pedler who came into the store—laid in a stock of matches, pencils, shoe-brushes, suspenders, bootjacks, and blacking, which will last me a short lifetime—bought so much candy that the office-boy had the colic every afternoon for a week—called the applewoman "my own sweet love," and said "thank you, darling," when she gave me pewter dimes in change.

Wrote spasmodic poetry about Calanthe's hair—lines to her raven tresses—stanzas to her locks of jet—odes to her ebon ringlets—verses to her sable curls—rhymes to her coal-black hair, and commenced a poem in 17 cantos, to her ebony-topped head, but on reflection I was led to doubt the propriety of the comparison.

Called to see her every evening—substantial victuals didn't agree with me—a kind word from her was a good breakfast—a tender glance has served me for a dinner many a time, and once when she pressed my hand I couldn't eat anything for a fortnight but oranges, cream-candy, and vanilla-beans.

We went to the theatre, endured the negro minstrels, and braved the horrors of a second-rate Italian Opera Company—in fact, everywhere, where there was anything to be seen or heard, there were Calanthe Maria, and her devoted Philander.

For a month I forgot my debts, neglected business, ignored entirely this mundane sphere, and lived in a rainbow-colored aerial castle, of the most elegant finish—surrounded by roses, attended by cupids, and just big enough for Calanthe Maria and the subscriber.

In that happy place there were no duns, no tailors' bills, no trouble, no debts, no getting up early cold mornings, no tight boots, no bad cigars: nothing but love, luxury, and Calanthe Maria.

Came down occasionally out of my airy mansion, to speak a few words of compassion to my companions in the office, who hadn't got any Calanthe, but I went right back again as quick as I could to that rose-colored dream-land where love and Calanthe were "boss and all hands."

At last, one fatal evening I was undeceived.

We were waltzing, and through some clumsiness on my part, her hair caught in a gas-fixture—some mysterious string broke, and those glossy ringlets, the object of my adoration, *came off*, leaving her head bald as a brickbat. Relating this scrape of the locks to a friend, he informed me that the rest of her charms would not bear minute inspection, for she wore false teeth, and bought her complexion at Phalon's; that her graceful form was the result of a skilful combination of cotton and whalebone.

This was too much. While I thought Calanthe a woman, I loved her, but the discovery of the *fishy* element excited a prejudice—as a *female*, she had my affection, and I contemplated matrimony—as a land mermaid, I had no desire to swindle Barnum and become her proprietor.

Coming as I did, from a section of the country where they have *human* women, and where they don't attempt to deceive masculine mankind with French millinery strategy, I was unprepared for counterfeits, and had been easily deluded by a spurious article. But I find that in New York, perambulating bundles of dry goods not unfrequently pass current as women—and the milliners now put their eccentric inventions upon these locomotive shams, to the great neglect of those revolving waxen ladies who used to perform their perpetual gyrations in the show-windows.

As an advertising medium, they possess facilities for publicity beyond any of the newspapers, having a city circulation, which is unattainable by anything dumb and unpetticoated.

The great staple of the south has not only "made" some of our first men, but has been discovered to enter largely into the composition of many of our first ladies.

My madness was now over—the intoxication of love was dissipated, and I was once more able to get about my business without having a feminine name constantly present to my eyes. The stages, the dry-goods' boxes, the streets and signs, were once more lettered in sensible characters. I was guilty of no more poetry, went to no more operas—in short, exhibited no longer any of the signs of insanity, but relapsed at once into my former unpoetical condition—the spell was broken—the blind fiend was exorcised—reason got back to her old bunk, and "Richard was himself again."

The difference in my mental condition occasioned

my landlady considerable alarm; while I had lived on love, and paid five dollars a week for the privilege of sitting down at table only, she had considered me a profitable boarder; but the disappearance of beef and substantials generally, consequent upon my returning appetite, sensibly diminish her esteem for me. I fancy I can perceive a change in her treatment, for she sets the bread and butter as far away from me as possible.

P. S.—She has raised my board to eight dollars a week, and with a consciousness that I deserve it, I submit.

## XV.

### Modern Patent Piety—Church-Going in the City.

PERSONS from the rural districts—who are visiting the city for the first time, and who have all their lives been accustomed to no more pretentious religious edifices than the old fashioned country meeting-house, with a "steeple," either of the extinguisher or pepper-castor pattern; with great square hot-house windows, built expressly to concentrate and reflect upon the innocent congregation the hottest rays of the sun, as if religion was a green-house plant, and would only bloom beneath a forced and artificial heat—usually expend no small portion of their simple wonder upon the magnificent temples of the town, which aspiring congregations erect ostensibly for the worship of the manger-cradled Saviour.

It usually too requires some considerable time for such a behind-the-times person to lay aside all his antiquated notions of religion, in which love, charity, and good will to men were essential elements, but which primitive idea of Christianity has, in the more enlightened city precincts, been long since exploded, and adopt the more convenient and showy piety which fashionable city people wear on Sundays—the constituent parts of which are too often only ostentation and vanity, veneered with a thin shell of decency and decorum. Such church-going people are remarkably easy on the Bible—most of the doctrines therein inculcated having been long since explained away by their three-thousand-dollar clergyman, who measures his people for their religion, and fits them with as much nicety as their tailors or dressmakers do in the case of more visible wardrobe. One or two Sundays after my first appearance in this town of patent Christianity, I attended service for the first time.

Having seen the opera with detestation, the theatres with approbation, George Christy with cachinnation, and No. 2 Dey street with affiliation; having visited Castle Garden, the model artists, and the American Museum; in fact, knowing something of almost all the other places of amusement in the city, I resolved to complete and crown my knowledge by going to church, and I hope I may receive due credit for my pursuit of amusement under difficulties. I made known my heroic determination to my new-found friends, and they instantly resolved to bear me company—Bull Dogge by way of variety, and Damphool from force of habit—(Bull Dogge seldom goes to church, and Damphool *always* does).

Sunday morning came, and the aforesaid individuals presented themselves—B. D. looked pugnacious and pugilistic, and Damphool perfectly marvellous—in fact, majestic as this latter-named person had ever borne himself, and importantly huge as he had ever appeared, his coat tails were now so wonderfully short, his collar so enviably large, and so independently upright, and his hat so unusually and magnificently lofty, that he certainly looked a bigger Damphool than ever before.

Walked up Broadway through a crowd of people of all sorts, sizes, colors, and complexions; countrymen running over every third man they met; New Yorkers threading their way through apparently un-get-thro'-a-ble crowds without ruffling their tempers or their shirt collars—(By the way, I have discovered that no one but a genuine New Yorker, born and bred, can cross Broadway upon a dignified walk;) firemen in red shirts, and their coats over their arms; newsboys with a very scanty allowance of shirt, and no coats at all; Dutch emigrants, with dirty faces, nasty breeches, and long loppy looking pipes; Irish emigrants, with dirtier faces, nastier breeches, and short, stubbier pipes; spruce-looking darkies, and wenches arrayed in rainbow-colored habiliments—and at last reached the door of the church.

For about a quarter of a mile on either side of the entrance there extended a row of carriages, lined with satin, with velvet cushions; and on every carriage there were a couple of men with white gloves on, gold bands round their hats, a black rosette on the side, and a short cloak over their shoulders, with cloth enough in the multitudinous capes of each to make a full suit of clothes for a common-sized man, and three or four half grown boys. Bull Dogge informed me that these were the liveried flunkies of our republican aristocracy, and that it was made their business to sit outside the church and watch the lazy over-fed horses, while their owners were inside saying American "amens" to democratic prayers that liberty and equality may be established over all the earth.

The coachman spends his Sabbath hours in the pious occupation of cracking his whip at the little boys who are playing marbles on the side-walk, reading the Sunday papers, and saying hard words at the flies which make his horses shake their nettings off—while the genteel footman goes to sleep in the carriage, with his boots out of the window, and only arouses from his slumber in time to open the door for my lady, as she comes from her courtly devotions.

We passed the scrutiny of these gentlemen without exciting any audible impertinence, and reached the door of the church. Everything looked so grandly gingerbready that I hesitated about going in. Little boy in the corner (barefooted, with a letter in the post-office) told us to "go *in*," and called us "*lemons*." Did not perceive the force of his pomological remark, but "*went in*" nevertheless. Man in a white cravat showed us to a pew; floor covered with carpet, and seat covered with damask, with little stools to kneel down upon. Bull Dogge says that at one time the prevailing style of pantaloons nearly caused a division in the church, which was however compromised by an alteration in the litany, and allowing the gentlemen to stand during the performance cf certain prayers instead of kneeling down, which latter feat was difficult of accomplishment, on account of the *tightness of their straps.* Some of the congregation were however so much offended that they stayed away, and used home-made prayers, instead of coming to church and dealing in the orthodox ready-made article.

Got inside; crowd of people; minister fenced up in a kind of back closet, in a pulpit trimmed with red velvet and gilt-edged prayer-books.

Pretty soon, music—organ—sometimes grand and solemn, but generally fast and lively enough for a contra-dance. (B. D. said the player got a big salary to show off the organ, and draw a big house.)

He commenced to play Old Hundred (Damphool suggests Ancient Century).

At first, majestic as it should be, but soon his left hand began to get unruly among the bass notes, then the right cut up a few monkey shines in the treble; left threw in a large assortment of quavers, right led off with a grand flourish and a few dozen variations; left struggled manfully to keep up, but soon gave out, dead beat, and after that went back to first principles, and hammered away religiously at Old Hundred, in spite of the antics of its fellow; right struck up a march, marched into a quick step, quickened into a gallop; left still kept at Old Hundred; right put in all sorts of fantastic extras, to entice the left from its sense of propriety; left still unmoved; right put in a few bars of a popular waltz; left wavers a little; right strikes up a favorite polka; left evidently yielding; right dashes into a jig; left now fairly deserts its colors and goes over to the enemy, and both commence an animated hornpipe, leaving poor Old Hundred to take care of itself.

Then with a crash, a squeak, a rush, a roar, a rumble, and an expiring groan, the overture concluded and service began.

First, a prayer; then a response; prayer; response; by the priest and people alternately, like the layers of bread and butter, and ham and mustard in a sandwich; then a little sing, then a little preach, then more petitions and more responses.

Damphool read the entire service, Minister's cues included, and sung all the hymns. I noticed that Bull Dogge gave all the responses with a great deal of energy and vigor. He said he always liked to come to this kind of Church, because when they jawed religion at him, he could jaw back.

Kept as cool as I could, but could not help looking round now and then to see the show.

Elderly lady on my right, very devout, gilt edged prayer-book, gold-covered fan, feathers in her bonnet, rings on her fingers, and for all I know, "bells on her toes."

Antiquated gentleman in same slip, well preserved but somewhat wrinkled, smells of Wall street, gold spectacles, gold-headed cane, put three cents in the plate.

Fashionable little girl on the left—two flounces on her pantalettes, and a diamond ring *over* her glove.

Young America looking boy, four years old, patent leather boots, standing collar, gloves, cane, and cigar case in his pocket.

Foppish young man with adolescent moustache, pumps, legs *à la* spermaceti candles, shirt front embroidered *à la* 2.40 race horse, cravat *à la* Julien, vest *à la* pumpkin pie, hair *à la* soft soap, coat-tails *à la* boot-jack, which when parted discovered a view of the Crystal Palace by gas-light on the rear of his pantaloons, wristbands *à la* stove pipe, hat *à la* wild

Irishman, cane to correspond; total effect *à la* Shanghae.

Artificial young lady, extreme of fashion; can't properly describe her, but here goes: whalebone, cotton, paint and whitewash; slippers *à la* Ellsler, feet *à la* Japanese, dress *à la* Paris, shawl *à la* eleven hundred dollars, parasol *à la* mushroom, ringlets *à la* corkscrew, arms *à la* broomstick, bonnet *à la* Bowery gal (Bull Dogge says the boy with buttons on him, brought it in, in a teaspoon, fifteen minutes after she entered the house), neck *à la* scrag of mutton, complexion *à la* mother of pearl, appearance generally *à la* humbug. (Bull Dogge offers to bet his hat, she don't know a cabbage from a new cheese, and can't tell whether a sirloin steak is beef, chicken, or fresh fish.)

At length, with another variette upon the organ, and all the concentrated praise and thanksgiving of the congregation, sung by four people up stairs, the service concluded. I thought from the manner of this last performance, each member of the choir imagined the songs of praise would never get to Heaven if he didn't give them a personal boost, in the shape of an extra yell.

Left the Church with a confused idea that the only way to attain eternal bliss, is to go to Church every Sunday, and to give liberally to the Foreign Missionary cause.

Bull Dogge tried to convince me, that one half the people present, thought that Fifth avenue runs straight into Heaven, and that their through tickets are insured, their front seats reserved, and that when they are obliged to leave this world, they will find a coach and four, and two servants in livery, ready to take them right through to the other side of Jordan.

# XVI.

## Benevolence Run Mad—Charitable Cheating.

I WAS so much affected by the services of the Church, had my feelings so much excited, and all my benevolent and charitable nature so thoroughly aroused by the sermon, that I felt an irresistible desire to rush out and give somebody something.

For I know that I am charitable; I feel it in my bones, like rheumatism. I always give money to the begwoman, who has such a large family at home; and to the whiny boy, with a club-foot, who asks charity in behalf of his sick mother.

True, I have seen the old lady when she was evidently inebriated, and apparently disposed to harangue the crowd in high Dutch—but then she was in excellent company; noble-looking men, with stars on their bosoms—and I have discovered that the club-footed boy changes all his money into cents, and gambles it away, playing "pitchpenny" in Theatre-alley; still, I keep on giving.

But it is also a fact that I am not always able to comply with the demands upon my purse. Twice have I been invited to "calico" parties, and at the bottom of each note was a modest request that I would make my appearance arrayed in such apparel only, as I would be willing to donate next day to the Five-Points Mission.

Could have done like the others—bought a ready-made coat and vest and given *them* with the greatest pleasure—but the hint in the invitation seemed to include the entire wardrobe brought into requisition on the occasion, and when I thought of a Five-Points darkey in my ruffled shirt and gold studs, I was "suddenly indisposed," and sent my "regrets."

But I did go to a ball for the benefit of the poor—a two-dollar commingling of "upper-tendom" with "lower-twentydom"—an avalanche of exclusiveness, in a torrent of mobocracy—where the crowd was so great that faces lost their identity, and I was only conscious of a hustling mass of dressed up humanity—a forest of broadcloth wrecked in an ocean of calico. I barely escaped with life, and reached home in a state of collapse

Afterward, went to a concert in behalf of the poor—where I sat all the evening in a hard seat with a number on the back, to see a woman make faces at a well-dressed audience, and sing music which I could not understand—the people all applauded when she screamed, and threw bouquets at her when she made a noise like a swamp-blackbird.

But after listening to the stirring address before alluded to, I felt that I had not done enough; so, obedient to the promptings of my impulsive nature, I determined to give something more, and being so far *cityfied* in my habits that I desired to combine amusement with charity, and only give my money to the needy after I had received its worth in dancing, got its full value in foreign music at a high price, or eaten its equivalent in oysters and ice-cream at some kind of a pseudo-charitable gathering, I looked about me for some fitting opportunity to bestow my charity on the deserving poor, after making it previously pay for some delectation for myself.

It did not take me long to find out that there was soon to be a ladies' fair, in aid of the poor, given by the benevolent ladies of the Church of the Holy Poker.

Damphool (who can't give up city associations, and who wouldn't read his Bible if it wasn't printed in New York) had sent to me from his rural solitude to procure him a dressing-gown, a pair of slippers, and a crocheted worsted comforter.

Thought I couldn't have a better opportunity to purchase these, and so I went to the fair.

Got to the hall, paid my twenty-five cents at the door, went in—saw plenty of long tables, with ladies behind them playing "keep store"—tables covered with mysterious articles of baby linen, and complicated pieces of female harness, designed for uses to me unknown, and also all sorts of impracticable unnecessaries intended for gentlemen.

Slippers that you couldn't get on; smoking caps that could never, by any possibility, fit anybody (shaped like a Chinese pagoda, and full of tinsel and spangles to make them prickly); cigar cases, that you couldn't get a cigar into without breaking both ends off (perhaps they expect us to smoke "stubs," like the newsboys); pin-cushions, stuffed so hard they would turn the point of a marlin-spike; watch cases, just big enough to hold a three cent piece; pen wipers, that fill the point of a pen full of wool—and divers other nonsensical inconveniences fabricated by speculating females, the patterns being always very short, and the stitches very long (I suppose they think we don't know the difference), to palm off upon victimized gentlemen; and these latter resignedly submit to a price so exorbitant, that if a Chatham-street Israelite had the impudence to ask it they'd straighten out his fish-hook nose like a darning needle.

The prettiest looking girls are always placed where the least attractive-looking merchandise is displayed, and they ask the biggest kind of prices, trusting to the gallantry of the gentlemen "not to beat them down," flattering themselves, I suppose, that their pretty looks are "value received" for the exchange.

One consequence of this arrangement is, that every buyer spends all the money he has in his purse, taking in exchange therefor a lot of stuff so utterly useless, and so ridiculously absurd, that after having it on his table for a week or so to laugh at, he is fain to get rid of the rubbish, by giving the whole to his chamber-maid.

Sometimes your purchases will hold together till you leave the room, and sometimes not; you must show yourself a man, and "equal to either fortune."

There was a post-office; pretty girl called me;

had a letter for me; bought it; paid ten cents; nothing in it—blank.

Solicitous young lady very anxious to have me give her twenty-five cents to tell me how much I weighed; paid her the money, and she told me within fifty-one pounds and a half.

Young woman wanted me to invest in the "grab bag;" gave half a dollar, and fished in; got, in three times trying, a tin whistle, half a stick of candy, and a peanut done up in tissue paper.

Went on to the auction table, where, after much competition with a ringleted miss (who was put there to make Peter Funk bids against probable purchasers), succeeded in bidding in a China vase, which I soon discovered had a hole in the bottom, and wouldn't hold water any more than it would bake pork. If I had bought it anywhere else should have thought I had been swindled, and have demanded my money back, but here I supposed it was an exemplification of some newly discovered principle of fair dealing with which I was not yet acquainted.

Was much amused with the way they disposed of the unsold goods—certain number of articles, (things left at the tables tended by the homely girls) and for each article twenty tickets were put into a hat, whence they were drawn out singly, and the last tickets drawn were to have the prizes—should have thought it was just the same as a lottery, if I had not been acquainted with the ladies, and known they wouldn't do anything so naughty.

Came to a place where an old lady, with steel spectacles, was cutting up a loaf of cake into particularly small pieces—asked what it meant—was told there was a gold ring somewhere in the cake, and they proposed to sell each piece for a quarter of a dollar, and give the ring to the lucky buyer—wondered if it wasn't another lottery on a small scale, but supposed it couldn't be—went to the supper-room.

It is a curious metropolitan fact, that at parties, balls, or wherever a refreshment-table is spread, every man seems to regard it as his duty to fill himself to the very lips with all the "delicacies of the season," and to accomplish it in the least time possible—as if he was a gun, and anxious to ascertain his calibre, and find out how quickly he could be loaded in case of necessity.

And the ladies are not far behind; this evening I learned how much a female *can* eat in a charitable cause.

A pale-faced ball-room belle is a modern Sphinx—a gastronomic problem, whose solution will probably never be satisfactorily expounded.

Under the impression that she would not eat more than I had money to pay for, I invited a lady to take some refreshments, and I certainly think that, like the countryman, she imagined she was bound to eat all the bill-of-fare called for.

She ate stewed oysters—fried oysters—boiled turkey with oyster sauce, celery—oysters on the shell—ice cream, sponge cake, and Charlotte russe—Roman punch, two water-ices, coffee, sandwiches, cold sausage, lobster salad, oysters broiled, also stewed again, and six on the shell—orange jelly, grape ditto, cake; she then hinted again at oysters, but as the supply had run out, she was obliged to go hungry—paid the bill with a certified check on the Merchants' Bank, which luckily covered the amount, and greatly relieved my mind; for I feared there would be a balance which I would have to give my note for.

Having previously procured the articles required for my friend, I immediately left—go home—got there, and proceeded to examine my purchases—found that the slippers—having been pasted together without the slightest regard to permanency, had come apart in my pocket, my comforter had ravelled out, so that I had about six inches comforter, and a wad of yarn big enough to make a horse blanket—my dressing-gown had been made of a moth-eaten remnant, and where there *was* any sewing, every stitch was as long as a railroad, but the sleeves had, I verily believe, been put in with court plaster, and the long seams closed with carpenter's glue.

Made up my mind that the objects of that feminine institution, a Ladies' Fair, are somewhat as follows:

Firstly, to give the ladies an opportunity to show their new clothes, and to talk with a multitude of unknown gentlemen, without any preliminary introduction.

Secondly, to beg as much moneyas possible from the gentlemen aforesaid, under the transparent formality of bargain and sale—which sale includes the buyer, who is really the only article fairly "sold" in the whole collection.

Thirdly, to give some money to the ostentatiously poor, if there is any left after paying expenses, and the Committee don't spend it in carriage-hire.

In New York, by a refinement in Benevolence,

engendered by the hardness of the times, and the necessity of making the money go as far as it will, charity money answers a double purpose; procuring pleasure for the rich, and soup for the poor.

Thus if you pay three dollars for a ticket to the Opera or Ball, you can enjoy your Aria, or Schottische, with a double relish; and can eat oysters and turkey, and gulp down creams and ices till your stomach "strikes," in the labor of love, with the happy consciousness, that it is all for "sweet charity"—and if the three dollars, before it reach the needy, in whose behalf you gave it, dwindles to three dimes and a fip, you can, knowing you have done *your* duty, poetically exclaim, with the noble Thane, "Thou can'st not say *I* did it."

## XVII.

### Millerite Jubilee—How they didn't go up.

IN company with many others of the same genus and who may be classed under the same general cognomen, my friend Damphool lately became convinced that according to the comfortable prediction of Mr. Miller, the "end of Earth" would become speedily visible to the naked eye, as that amiable gentleman had advertised the world to burn on the nineteenth day of May, 1855. According to the programme, the entertainment was to commence with a trumpet solo by Gabriel (not the one of City Hall celebrity), to be followed by a general "gittin' up stairs," and grand mass meeting of the illustrious defunct—after which "the elect" were to start for Paradise in special conveyances provided for their accommodation —the whole to conclude with a splendid display of fireworks in the evening.

Damphool had done nothing but sing psalms for a

week. Bull Dogge, who was also a convert, had packed up his wardrobe in a hat-box, and left the city; saying that he owned forty shares in a Kentucky coal mine, and was going to take possession of his property; and he offered to bet us the drinks that if he stood on a vein of *that* coal, he would be the last man scorched.

Damphool squared up his board bill, and paid his washerwoman, which left him dead broke; sold his watch to a "blaspheming Jew" to raise money with which to procure an ascension robe; in order to do honor to the occasion, he got one made of linen cambric; it was a trifle too long, and cut him malignantly under the arms, but he bore it like a martyr; he got shaved, took a bath, put on his robe, bid me farewell, and got ready to go up.

I discovered the place from which they were to start, and went up myself to see the operation—in a vacant lot, where there were no trees to catch their skirts in their anticipated flight—large crowd on the ground.

One maiden lady in a long white gown, had also dressed her lap-dog in a similar manner.

Man with a family Bible in his hand, had forgotten his robe, and come in his shirt-sleeves.

Ancient wench in a white night-gown, with red shoes, and a yellow handkerchief round her head, knelt down in a small puddle of rain water, and prayed to take her up easy, and not hurt her sore ancle.

Lady from East Broadway, came in a robe cut low in the neck, and trimmed with five flounces.

Red-haired woman made her appearance with a crying baby, to the consternation of the company, who expected to go to Heaven, and had no relish for a preliminary taste of the other place.

Careful old lady, brought her overshoes in a work-basket, to wear home in case the performance should be postponed.

Little girl, had her doll, and her three year old brother had a hoop, a tin whistle, and a painted kite.

Poor washerwoman came, but as she had only a cotton robe, and a scant pattern at that, the more aristocratic ladies moved farther away, and smelt their cologne, while the poor woman knelt down in the corner, with her face to the fence.

Sixth Avenue lady came in a white satin robe; had a boy to hold up her train, and she had her own hands full of visiting cards.

An African brunette carried a cushion for her

mistress to kneel upon, and a man followed behind with a basket containing her certificate of church membership, a gilt-edged prayer-book, two mince-pies and some ham sandwiches.

Old cripple hobbled up, and as he was devoutly saying his prayers, a bad boy (who had not made any preparation for aerial travelling) stole his crutch to make a ball club.

Crowd began to separate into knots, according to their different creeds and beliefs; Unitarians, Baptists, Presbyterians, and Methodists, clustering round their respective preachers.

I noticed that one old lady, evidently believing in the perfect sanctity of her darling minister, and desiring to insure her own passage, had tied herself to his left leg with a fish line.

Baptist man was preaching close communion.

Presbyterian man was descanting on the accountability of infants, and asserting that a child three years old can commit sufficient sin to doom it to the lowest hell.

Sunrise—all knelt down to pray; east wind blew, and it began to rain. I noticed that Damphool had found a dry place on the lee side of a cider barrel.

Methodist man took off his coat, and made a

stump prayer, while all his congregation yelled "*Glory.*"

Baptist man inserted a special clause in his supplication, that he and his crowd might go up in a separate boat.

Ministers all prayed *at* each other, and *for* nobody.

Know-Nothing clergyman addressed a long-winded political prayer to the Almighty, detailing the latest election returns, deploring the choice of the opposition candidate, imploring his blessing on the next governor (if the world *should* stand), insinuated that he expected the nomination himself, and concluded by advising Him to exclude from heaven all foreigners, or they would refuse to live up to the regulations, and would certainly kick up another row among the celestials.

Down-town man, on hand, ready to go up; tried to pray, but from want of practice, could only utter some disjointed sentences about "uncurrent funds," "money market," "Erie down to 36;" (Damphool whispered that if *that* man ever got to heaven he would melt down the golden harp into coin, and let it out at two per cent. a month.)

Began to rain harder; wind decidedly chilly; their teeth chattered with cold, and they began to wish for the conflagration to commence. Naughty boys on the fence began to throw stones—promiscuous praying on every side. Anxious man stopped in the midst of a long, touching supplication to cuff the ears of a little boy who hit him with a brick; hours slipped away, began to think the entertainment was "postponed on account of the weather."

Noon came; folks were not half so scared as they were in the morning; ministers had got too hoarse to talk, and were passing the time kissing the sisters.

Damphool looked so chilly that I got him a glass of hot whiskey punch; he looked at me with holy horror, and went on with his prayer, but before he got to "amen," the punch had disappeared.

Husband of red-haired woman came and ordered her to go home and wash the breakfast dishes and then mend his Sunday pantaloons.

One o'clock, zeal began to cool off; at two the enthusiasm was below par; at three the rain poured so that I thought an alteration in the Litany would be necessary to make it read, "Have mercy upon us miserable *swimmers*." Small boy threw a handful of gravel at long man, which hit him in the face, and made him look like a mulatto with the small-pox. Long man punched small boy with a fence rail.

Four o'clock; Gabriel hadn't come yet. Damphool, much disappointed, muttered something about being "sold;" people evidently getting hungry; no loaves or fishes on the ground; woman with two children said she was going home to put them in the trundle-bed; long man looked round to see that no one was looking, then tucked his robe under his arm, got over the fence, and started for home on a dog trot.

Dark; no signs of fireworks yet; pyrotechnic exhibition not likely to commence for some time. Crowd impatient. (I here missed Damphool, and found him an hour afterwards, paying his devotions to an eighteen-penny oyster stew and a mug of ale.)

Stayed an hour longer, when the crowd began to disperse, with their ascension robes so sadly draggled, that if they HAD received a second summons to go, it would have taken an extra quantity of soap-suds to make them presentable among decent angels.

Appointed myself a committee of five to inquire into the matter; offered the following resolution, which I unanimously adopted:—

*Resolved*, That putting on a clean shirt to go to heaven in, don't always result in getting there, even though the tails be of extra length, and that the creed which teaches such a mode of procedure is a farcical theology, fully worthy to be ranked among the many other excellent "sells" of that veteran joker of world-wide celebrity—*Jo Miller*.

# XVIII.

## The Great "American Tragedian."

THE only dramatic performances known in the wild region where I passed some of my early years, are given by companies of strolling players who usually give their classic entertainments in a barn, have a piece of carpet for a drop curtain, four tallow candles for footlights, and who generally go out of town in the night without paying their Tavern bills.

Almost every Drama performed by them, requires more people to represent it than are contained in the entire troupe; the services of a crowd of aspiring country boys are secured for soldiers, citizens, robbers, and other personages who don't have to say anything; but there is still a large gap which can only be filled by the "doubling" of several parts by one performer. Hence it is by no means unusual in the "tragedy of Richard III." to see King Henry,

The Great "American Tragedian."

after being deliberately despatched by Gloster in the first act, reappear in the second as the Duke of Buckingham, and then, after his supposed decapitation in obedience to the ferocious order of Richard, "Off with his head," come back in the final scenes, equipped in a full suit of mail, as the Earl of Richmond, and avenging his double murder by killing the "crook-backed tyrant" with a broadsword after a prolonged struggle.

And in Macbeth, King Duncan, after being carved up by his treacherous kinsman with two white handled butcher-knives, returns as Hecate in the witch scenes, and afterwards as court physician to Lady M., besides which he generally blows the flourishes on the trumpet for the entrances of the King, beats the bass drum, and attends to the sheet-iron thunder.

I have always had a passion for theatricals, and was at one time of my variegated existence much more intimately connected with the stage than at present—and on reaching this city I felt, of course, a great desire to behold again the theatre, with all its brilliant fascinations—the light, the music, the varied scenery comprising gardens, chambers, cottages, mountains, "cloud-capped towers and gorgeous palaces," bar-rooms, churches, huts and hovels —to look again upon the glass jewels, the tinselled robes of mimic royalty, the pasteboard banquets and molasses wine, and all the glory, " pride, pomp and circumstance" and humbug which I once " knew so well," " *et quorum magna pars fui.*"

So, with my trusty friends, Damphool and Bull Dogge, I wended my way to the Metropolitan Theatre No. 1, to see and hear the distinguished Mr. Rantanrave Hellitisplit, the notorious American tragedian, in his great, original, unapproachable, inconceivable, inexplicable, incomprehensible part of " What a bore O, the last of the Vollypogs."

I had heard so much of this great actor in this particular part, that I expected to behold nothing less than the " Eighth wonder of the world."

Opera glasses were continually levelled at us by people who, impelled by a laudable curiosity, were anxious to see all that could *be* seen. (Damphool says, that when you see a *woman* with one of these implements, you may be sure she wants to be looked at—and called my attention to the confirmatory fact, that all the ladies with the finest busts, and the best developed forms, wore their dresses the lowest in the neck, and sported the biggest opera glasses). (Bull

Dogge asserts that they were invented by the author of "Staring made Easy," and "A Treatise on the Use of Globes.")

After a season of tramping by the intelligent audience, which seemed, by its measured regularity, to intimate that they had learned the motion in the treadmill, the bell jingled and the members of the orchestra entered, one by one.

The audience endured the prolonged tuning of the instruments, conducted in a masterly manner by the leader of the band, the music got "good ready" for a fair start, and at the word "go" they went.

Could not critically analyse the uproar, but it seemed to be composed of these elements: a predominance of drum and cymbals—a liberal allowance of flute and horn—a spasmodic sprinkling of trombone—a small quantity of oboe, and a great deal of fiddle. The tumult was directed by the leader, who waved the fiddle over his head, jumped up and down upon his seat, kicked up his heels, disarranged his shirt collar, threw his arms wildly about, stamped, made faces, and conducted himself as if he was dancing a frantic hornpipe for the gratification of the crazy whims of an audience of Bedlamites.

At length the curtain went up—two men came on

and said something, then two others came on and did something—then the scene changed, and some others came on and listened to a shabby-looking general, who seemed to be their " magnus Apollo" and who certainly was very long-winded.

Nothing decisive, however, came to pass until the long-expected entrance of the great Hellitisplit himself eventuated.

I must confess that I was awed by the terrific yet serene majesty of his appearance. When I saw the tragic, codfishy expression of his eyes, I was surprised; when I observed the flexibility of his capacious mouth, opening and shutting, like a dying mudsucker, I was amazed. When my eye turned to his fingers, which worked and clutched, as if feeling for coppers in a dark closet, I was wonder-stricken—but when my attention was called to the magnitude of his legs, I was fairly electrified with admiration, and could not forbear asking Bull Dogge if those calves were capable of locomotion.

What-a-bore-O, is supposed to be an Indian Chief, and although it is the prevailing impression that Indians are beardless, the face of this celebrated performer proved this opinion to be a physiological fallacy.

For upon his chin he wore a tuft of hair, a round black hirsute knob, neither useful nor ornamental, but which looked as if somebody had hit him in the face with a blacking-brush, and a piece had stuck to his lower jaw.

The admiring audience, who had kicked up perfect young earthquake when he came on, only ceased when he squared himself, put out his arm and prepared to speak.

That voice! Ye Gods! that voice! It went through gradations that human voice never before attempted, imitating by turns the horn of the City Hall Gabriel, the shriek of the locomotive, the soft and gentle tones of a forty-horse-power steam sawmill, the loving accents of the scissor-grinder's wheel, the amorous tones of the charcoal-man, the rumble of the omnibus, the cry of the driver appertaining thereto—rising from the entrancing notes of the infuriated house-dog to the terrific cry of the oyster vender—causing the "supes" to tremble in their boots, making the fiddlers look around for some place of safety, and moving the assembled multitude to echo back the roar, feebly, it is true, but still with all their puny strength.

(Bull Dogge says he got that awful voice by

eating pebble-stone lunches, like the man in the book.)

Several times during the piece I was much affected —when he wound his arms round his wife, stuck his head over her shoulder, and kissed the back of her neck—when he made a grand exit, with three stamps, a hop, a run, and two long straddles—when he talked grand about the thunder, shook his fist at the man in the flies—when he killed the soldiers in the council room, shouted for them to "come one and all," and then ran away for fear they would—when he swore at the man who did not give him his cue—when he knelt down and said grace over his dead boy, and then got up and stuck his wife with the butcher-knife; but at no part of the whole piece was I so impressed with his pathetic power, his transcendent genius, as when he laid his hand solemnly on his stomach, and said "What a bore, O cannot lie!" (Damphool asked, in a whisper, if Othello's occupation was gone).

And at the death scene, when he was shot, I was again touched to the heart; first he wabbled about like a top-heavy liberty pole in a high wind; then he stuck out one leg, and wiggled it, after the manner of a galvanic bull-frog; then sat down on the floor, opened his eyes and looked around; then grappled an Indian on one side, clutched a soldier on the other, struggled to his feet, staggered about like a drunken Dutchman, made a rush forwards, then a leap sideways, stiffened out like a frozen pig, collapsed like a wet dish-cloth, exerted himself till his face was the color of an underdone beefsteak, then sank back into the arms of the Indians, whispered to let him down easy, rolled up the whites of his eyes, settled himself to die—concluded to have a parting curse at the surrounding people, took a long swear, laid down, and with a noise in his throat like castanets, a couple of vigorous kicks and a feeble groan, gave up the ghost.

Bull Dogge asserted that he would resuscitate, brush the dust off his legs (take some gin and sugar, and come out and make a speech), all of which he did; the butcher boys in the gallery (Damphool says Hellitisplit commenced life as a respectable butcher-boy, but has degenerated into the man he is,) gave three cheers, Hellitisplit opened his mouth four times, shut it thrice (he went off with it wide open), and backed off with a grace which we may suppose would be exhibited by a mudturtle on the tight rope.

Damphool was in ecstacies—Bull Dogge asked me how I liked the "great American," &c." I replied that I knew not which most to admire, his euphonious voice, or his tremendous straddle, but that (notwithstanding the late appropriation of the name by a rival show-shop), I was ready to maintain with the butcher boys that there was but one Metropolitan Theatre, an l Hellitisplit is its profit.

# XIX.

## "Side Shows" of the City.

WE are all aware that Chatham Street and the Bowery are the legitimate abiding places of those benevolent Hebrews, whose zeal for the public welfare, and pity for ragged humanity, lead them to continually offer their valuable and undoubtedly durable articles of wearing apparel to the needy public "below cost;" and the enviable philosophy with which they bear the "alarming sacrifices" which must daily deplete their ample fortunes, has often been the subject of wondering remark.

The question, what becomes of these philanthropic tradesmen after their ultimate impoverishment, which of course must speedily supervene, is a fruitful subject for the investigation of some inquisitive mind. The charitable supposition is, that as soon as their pecuniary ruin is effectually accomplished, they retire to the shades of private life, happy in the consciousness of having done their little utmost to benefit the human race; seeing in each well dressed man, a perambulating monument of their beneficence, and in each ragged urchin, cause of regret that their altered circumstances cannot afford him a better pair of breeches.

But these Israelitish avenues before mentioned, are not only the headquarters of these philanthropic gentlemen, but are the depot for many other imitations of humanity, and curious specimens of human skill unknown to the unobserving.

Here abound those impassive wooden Indians of some tribe extinct, save in these civilized localities, who stand in the doors of seven by nine tobacco-factories, offering in persevering silence perpetual bunches of basswood cigars to the passer-by.

Here are plentifully sprinkled multitudes of three-cornered shops where patient and eager women, so sharp and shrewd at a bargain, that he who buys must have all his wits about him, offer for sale the most incongruous assortment of second-hand property; from a last year's newspaper to a complete library, from a pint-cup to a seventy ton yacht, from a brass night-key to a steam-engine.

Here too, almost every other doorway is ornamented with daguerreotypes of distinguished personages—negro-dancers duly equipped with banjo, tamborine and clappers—militia officers rigged out in all the glory of feathers and tinsel—supreme rulers of Know-Nothing Lodges, resplendent in the full regalia of that astute and sapient order—and whole dozens of pictures of the beauteous model artists who exercise their modest calling in that vicinage; whose names are fanciful enough, but whose physical embellishments are not always the ones commonly attributed to the mythical characters they represent.

"Kitty Clover" with splay-feet and dirty silk tights as "Venus Rising from the Sea," "Lilly Dale" cross-eyed and knock-kneed, as the "Greek Slave"—"Kate Kearney," with eyes rolled up, mock-pearls in her hair, in an attitude which must be exceedingly trying, as "Morning Prayer," or a trio of clumsy squaw-like damsels with smirking faces and stumpy limbs, as the "Three Graces."

Not only are all these works of art exhibited gratis by the public-spirited habiters of Chatham Street and the Bowery, but they have an infinity of other exhibitions, which cannot be classified as either gratuitous, theatrical, or amphitheatrical, to see which a fee is demanded, moderate but peremptory, trifling but inevitable.

These consist principally of ferocious beasts captured by heroic men, and brought from their native fastnesses to astonish the city people—of deformed and monstrous beings which should be human, but whom nature has sent into the world destitute of arms or legs, or vital organs, the lack of which makes these curtailed individuals objects of wonder, of mystery, and of three-cent speculation—and of various animals, human and otherwise, trained to perform unheard of feats of strength, agility, or juggling sleight.

The whereabouts of these interesting prodigies is made known by huge paintings on nobody-knows-how-many square yards of canvass; and generally by a decrepit hurdy-gurdy played in a masterly manner by the enterprising proprietor, who occasionally varies his performance by reciting at the top of his voice the leading attractions of his exhibitions, and extending to the bystanders a general invitation to walk in, and get their money's worth.

Reader, whose dainty musical and dramatic tastes, our theatrical and operatic managers fail to gratify;

who have laughed your fill at Burton, and at Forrester; who have tired of Vestvali, Steffanone, D'Ormy, and the rest; who have grown sick of Badiali, impatient of Brignoli, and tired of both; who have ceased to interest yourself in the "Happy Family" either at the Academy of Music or at Barnum's; whose sickened ear is fatigued with the burnt-cork lyrics of Christy, Buckley, and their sooty accomplices in questionable harmonies; you, who know every inch in the circle of fashionable amusement, and long for some novelty to break the monotony of the tedious track; pray discard the Shanghae coat, don a more sensible and less noticeable garb, step from the Broadway sphere to the Bowery precincts, and there look upon wonders hitherto unknown, and which will heartily astonish your bewildered optics.

Let us begin with the Anacondas, and the "only living Rhinoceros;" let me speak, and you hold your breath, and marvel.

Pause ere you enter the apartment containing these prodigies of Natural History—these dread-inspiring denizens of the mighty rivers and impenetrable morasses of the tropics, examine carefully the gorgeous painting which decks the outside of the building.

How majestic in design! how masterly in the execution! Criticism is silent, and we can only speak to commend.

Observe the brilliancy of the coloring; the vivid red and yellow spots upon the serpents, which wind their powerful folds about that noble charger—(you thought it was a windmill? No, Sir! I have inspected it carefully, and I am positive it is intended for a horse.)

See with what an air of stolid placidity, and sleepy complacency, his rider, the gallant Indian Chief (you took him for the "Fat Boy"?—the mistake is perhaps excusable, but it is *not* the "Fat Boy,") draws his arrow to the head to pierce the slimy monster; (arrow? you imagined it a fish pole? wrong, my friend, palpably wrong, the instrument may suggest fish-pole, but it is undoubtedly meant for arrow;) whose tail, the artist, with a noble disregard of the principles of perspective which stamps him as an original genius, has caused to rest upon a mountain twenty miles in the distance.

Notice how the other monstrous reptile has twined himself in the branches of the palm-tree—(it looks like a hickory-broom. No, sir! "it is no such thing"—it is most emphatically a tree—) and with his fiery tongue, thrust from his gaping jaws, (of course it's a tongue, and you need not assert that it resembles a barber's pole with the end split up, for it doesn't,) is about to make a frightful descent upon the other steed. (*Another* horse? Yes, sir! another horse, although you assert it to be meant for a cider barrel on a three-legged stool.)

Admire the elegant yet terrible proportions of the mighty Rhinoceros, as he stalks majestically through the tall jungle-grass (you thought that was a terrier dog looking for rats in a barn-yard, did you? Well, my friend, the resemblance certainly is striking, but do not disparage the artist, who is undoubtedly much more familiar with terrier dogs than with the other brutes, and don't find fault with the Rhinoceros because he isn't bigger than a dog, for you perceive that if he had been represented the proper size he would have covered up the snakes, hidden the Indian from our sight, and rendered the landscape invisible.)

We pay our money and go inside. What, though, upon seeking the realization of this promise of novelty, instead of the living rhinoceros we see only the dried and shrivelled skin of what was probably once a hog? and the ferocious reptiles of fabulous size shrink into a couple of exaggerated angleworms?

Let us not find fault with the showman who is only carrying on a popular business on too small a scale to be honest. He should increase his stock of curious swindles, tell bigger stories and more of them, humbug a hundred people where now he swindles one, and so make his business honest and respectable.

Our attention is next claimed by the man without any arms, who is advertised to possess tremendous strength, and can do more things with his feet than most people can with their hands; who can draw, paint, load a gun, play the piano, violin, and accordeon, cut likenesses, put on a clean collar, shave himself, tell fortunes, set type, and saw wood.

Do not grumble if, instead of an admirable Crichton, whose accomplishments are to provoke your envy, you see only a miserable cripple, necessitated by poverty and inability to work, to make an exhibition of his deformity, and the poor devices to which he is driven, to supply, in some slight degree, the absence of his limbs.

Don't forget to see the "Living Skeleton," who has seen two score years, only weighs twenty ounces, and is so thin that when he is undressed he is invisible to the naked eye.

Visit also the dancing bears, the performing dogs, the wax figures, the mineralogical, geological, and conchological collections; see the female minstrels; the alligators, who have devoured in their native country an army of men, a multitude of women, and a myriad of nigger pickaninnies; see the magician who turns chickens into mugs of ale, and transmutes iron soup kettles into purest gold; the girl who dances a hornpipe on a drum-head, amongst a dozen eggs and never breaks any; the man who swallows a sword for his dinner, and lunches daily on jack-knives and gimlets; the boy who can tie his legs in a bow-knot on the back of his neck.

Go to see the individual who balances a ladder on the end of his nose, and his canine friend, who courageously ascends to the top thereof, and barks defiance to the world,—the juggler who tosses the balls and butcher knives,—the Chinaman who throws flip-flaps by the dozen, and makes a human cart-wheel of himself in the air, between heaven and earth, like Mahomet's coffin;—the learned Canary-birds which draw water, fire off guns, ring bells, and cut up all sorts of unnatural antics to earn their daily cuttlefish bone and loaf sugar; take a regular round of Bowery three cent amusements, glut your taste for novelty, take the edge off your curiosity, laugh at the bombastic humbugs enough to last you for a month; and then when the conglomeration of unaccustomed sights and sounds has tired out your aristocratic senses, go back to the Fifth Avenue world again, convinced that all the fun of the city is not located in Broadway or Chambers Street, or all the humbug concentrated between the City Hall Square and Maiden Lane

## XX.

### New Year's Day in New York.

THE last New Year's day previous to the one herein spoken of, was passed by the subscriber on board a Mississippi steamboat—said boat being fast aground on a sand-bar—provisions all gone—the captain, steward, and one of the bar-keepers being occupied playing "poker" with the passengers at one end of the boat, while the more piously disposed were listening to the drawling tones of a nautical preacher, who was discoursing second-hand sanctimony at the other—crew all on a "bender" in the engine room, firemen all drunk on the boiler deck, and every body generally enjoying themselves.

Made no calls, myself, except at the bar, where I wished myself so many happy New Years, and so many compliments of the season, that I slept that night on a pile of cotton-wood, and when I attained my state-room, next day, I found each berth occupied by a colored fireman, both with their boots on; one with my Sunday coat under his head for a pillow, his hair decorated with sundry lumps of stone-coal, and his red flannel shirt ornamented with the contents of a tar-bucket, and the carpenter's glue-pot.

Since that eventful time, I have become a sojourner in town, and on the approach of New Year's, had felicitated myself on the prospect of seeing how New Yorkers celebrate this universal holiday.

Intended to call on my friends, and hoped, as the number of my feminine acquaintances in this immediate vicinity is small, to get through in time to spend the afternoon at my new boarding-house, where Mrs. Griggs, my landlady, and her two daughters were to receive calls, and who had invited me to be present and see "the elephant" as far as the proceedings of the day should disclose to an unsophisticated eye, his mighty and magnificent proportions.

Early in the morning, dyed my incipient but dilatory moustache into visibility, dressed myself as fashionably as the resources of my limited wardrobe would permit, and, attended by my fast friend Sandie, started on my journey, intending to "fetch up" eventually at my boarding-house, "stopping at all the intermediate posts by the way."

A word about my friend Sandie. I have become much attached to him, from his strong resemblance in habits to the "fat boy" of the Pickwick papers. *He sleeps every where.*

In the omnibus, on the ferry-boat, in the store, at the Post-Office, in church, at the theatre, and even while walking along Broadway.

I have known him stop twenty-one stages in the course of an afternoon's walk by nodding at the drivers while he was enjoying a peripatetic nap. The first time I saw him I was the humble instrument of preserving his valuable existence. He had started to go to the Post-Office to mail an important letter, but had fallen asleep in Nassau street, and the bill-stickers had nearly overlaid him with show-bills, announcing that at the Bowery Theatre would be played the drama of the "Seven Sleepers," to be followed by the song "We 're all a Nodding," the whole to conclude with the farce "Rip Van Winkle."

In fact, he sleeps every where, except at table.

Open his sleepy eyes to the prospect of something good to eat, and his wakefulness will be insured until the uttermost morsel is entombed in those regions of unknown capacity to which he diurnally sends such astonishing quantities of provisions.

His internal dimensions have long been a favorite theme of speculation to his friends, but, alas! the problem must ever set at defiance all the ordinary rules of mensuration.

He has occasional fits of spasmodic piety, and then tries to read his Bible, and invariably goes to sleep and lets the book fall into the ashes—and I verily believe, that though his eternal salvation depended upon his reading three chapters of the Gospel without having a fit of somnambulism, he would go fast asleep before he had accomplished three verses.

Put ourselves into our new clothes and started on our tour. Went to the Smiths, Thompsons, Tompkins, Greens, Browns, Wiggins, Robinsons, &c.; in all these places there was the same performance, without change of programme. I give the formula—

Enter—speak to the lady of the house—"happy New Year," compliments—happy returns—take a glass of wine with the ladies—another of brandy or punch with the father—nibble a little cake—exit—to be repeated "*ad libitum.*"

At Jones' they had, on a side-table, a plate under a placard labelled "for the poor"—and every visitor was expected to drop in a contribution.

Some malicious person has recollected that the Joneses did the same thing last year, and his inconvenient and libellous memory has also recalled the circumstance that soon after New Year's, the two daughters of Jones had new silk dresses, and Mrs. J. rejoiced in a new cloak and hat of the richest style, and he says that Brogley, the broker, told him that on the 3rd of January last, Jones got some "tens" and "twenties" of him in exchange for small money, and made him give him two per cent. over because so much of it was silver change—and, in fact, he insinuates that as the money was to be "for the poor," Jones voted himself as poor as any body, and kept the proceeds—and rumor whispers that the Joneses won't have half so many calls this year as last, because their friends object to being taxed to pay their milliners' bills.

At Snooks' we found the doors closed, and a basket hung outside, in which to deposit cards—thought of the foundling hospital, &c.

Odd circumstance, very—but in all the parlors we visited that day I noticed one unvarying peculiarity of furniture—there were in no single parlor any two chairs of the same pattern—but they were of all shapes, sizes, dimensions, capacities, and degree of discomfort—from the damask-covered to the unvarnished, which looked as if they had strayed in from the kitchen. The effect of this arrangement is to impress a stranger with the idea that the owner of the establishment has been compelled to furnish his drawing-room from the chaotic assortment of a second-hand furniture store.

And, notwithstanding the recent election of a Maine Law Governor, in nearly every house, wines, brandy, punches, "hot stuff," and various inebriating drinks abounded, and every guest was compelled, on pain of slighting his host, to partake—the inevitable result was, that before night, many a youth, whose head might have withstood the attack of a single bottle, not being able to endure a twenty hours' siege, gave in dead-drunk—while others of harder heads and stronger stomachs, reeled from parlor to parlor, proclaiming the obituary of their respectability and decency, by exhibiting the noisy clamor, or idiotic gibber of beastly drunkenness, to the refined and polished ladies of "our best society"—in many cases rewarding the pseudo-hospitality of their fair entertainers by liberally sprinkling the marble steps to their noble mansions, with an unclean baptism from their aristocratic stomachs.

Kept Sandie awake until we entered a hack, and then let him relapse into a refreshing slumber, which continued until we reached home—entered the parlor, and took a seat in a corner, from which, unobserved, I could get a fair view of the various performances.

Every young lady is skilled in music, and an "elegant player" upon that tortured instrument, the piano—each can sing an assortment of "glees" from beautiful operas—transposing her voice into a vocal cork-screw, and opening her mouth so that, as a general thing, you can see those unmentionable articles, which are used, in fireman's phraseology, to "light up the hose"—and these songs, these delectable morsels of harmony, varied by such extemporaneous discords as the agitation or forgetfulness of the moment may occasion, are always "executed" for the entertainment of evening visitors.

Mrs. Griggs' daughters are no exception to this general rule.

First call—bell rings—enter bashful young man—evidently his first attempt at a fashionable visit—

came in with his hat in his hand—put it behind him to make his bow—dropped it—tried to pick it up—stepped in it—put his foot through it—fell over it—and in his frantic struggles to recover himself, burnt his coat, fractured his pantaloons, untied his cravat, demolished his shirt collar, and was finally borne away to the hall by his sympathizing friends; minus his patent moustache, one-half of which was afterwards found in Laura Matilda's scrap-book and the rest discovered in the coal-scuttle.

Crowd of young men came in together, (it is customary here, for young gentlemen to club their funds, hire a carriage by the hour, and go calling in a drove; stopping at every house where one of the company happens to be acquainted; so that when a lady keeps open house, for every person whom she knows or desires to see, a dozen unknown individuals annoy her by their uninvited presence,)—every one asked the young ladies to sing, and the young ladies *did* sing—generally opera, but sometimes varying the entertainment with the touching ballad of "Old Dog Tray," or the graceful and genteel melody, "Jordan is a Hard Road."

On this occasion the programme was somewhat as follows:—Gent. No. 1 was treated with a "gem from

Norma"—No. 2, a Grand March—No. 3, "Old Dog Tray"—No. 4, "Prima Donna Waltz"—No. 5, "Norma"—No. 6, "Jordan"—No. 7, "Norma"—No. 8, "Prima Donna," again—No. 9, "Norma"—No. 10, "Norma"—No. 11, "Dog Tray"—No. 12, "Norma," &c.; "Norma" being always ahead, and evidently a favorite of the field.

I have no doubt that in the whole city, yesterday, "Norma" must have been entreated to "hear my prayer," at least fifteen thousand distinct times, by probably five thousand imploring females—and these harmonious supplications, if blended and consolidated into one powerful, entreating scream, would have been sufficient to raise the ancient Druids from their graves, only to find that, although the final trump had not sounded, it was by an imitation by no means to be despised, that they had been fooled into a premature resurrection.

As evening came on, the guests who came showed signs of the day's indulgences—I was particularly edified by the movements of three of them, whom I noted with peculiar care—the first shook hands cordially with the servant girl, called her "Mrs. Griggs," wished her many happy returns, and on being told of his error, made an humble apology to the piano stool, and immediately sat down in a spittoon.

The next made his bow to the hat-stand in the hall, swaggered into the room, called for a brandy "smash"—tried to rectify his mistake by begging pardon of Mrs. G. for mistaking her parlor for a bar-room, and assured her, if he had done anything he was sorry for, he was exceedingly glad of it.

The third stumbled on to the sofa, and, after steadily contemplating his boots with much satisfaction for fifteen minutes, he picked up a Chinese fire-screen, and with an irresistible drunken sobriety, he tried to decipher the mysterious characters inscribed thereon, at the same time calling the attention of Mrs. G. to the capital story in "the Magtober number of Harper's Octazine."

Refreshments—first man often essaying to wipe his nose with his umbrella, which he afterwards placed in the music rack—poured his coffee into his ice-cream, put his cake and sandwich into its place, stirred them up with a tea-spoon, and tried to drink —the effort resulting in a signal failure, he passed his cup to the chandelier for "a little more sugar."

The next spilled his wine in Laura Matilda's neck, begged she wouldn't apologize, and offered to wipe it with his pocket handkerchief—by which appellation he designated the door mat, which he had brought in with him from the hall.

The other, after carefully depositing his plate on the floor, dropped his gloves into his saucer, and tried to put his over-coat into his vest pocket, made a great attempt to eat his cup of coffee with his knife and fork, and then resolutely set about picking his teeth with the nut-cracker.

After some complicated manœuvring, they bowed themselves out as best they could—but the last one, having mistaken the door and gone down cellar, instead of out-doors, was found next morning reposing complacently in the coal-hole.

In fact, New York, every New Year's Eve, goes to bed with a huge brick in its municipal hat, and, as the legitimate effect of such indiscretion, awakes next morning with a tremendous corporate headache —"Young America," for once, is unstarched in appearance; and in deportment, meek as the sucking dove.

## XXI.

### Amusement for the Million—A 2.40 Sleigh-ride.

SLEIGH-RIDING is an amusement to which I was never partial, for I cannot appreciate the pleasure there is, in a man's deliberately freezing his feet, and congealing his fingers into digital icicles; and for my own part unless there was some unusual charm beyond the ride itself, I would as soon think of seeking an evening's amusement by sitting a given number of hours on a frozen mill pond with my pedal extremities stuck through a hole in the ice into the water below. And in the city there are even more discomforts attending this popular penance than in the open country.

The man who would trustingly endeavor to draw a sherry cobbler out of a clam-shell, make a gin sling from cold potatoes, lard oil from railroad spikes, or a mint-julep out of sea weed and chestnut burs—or hopefully essay the concoction of a satisfactory oyster stew from jack-knife-handles and bootlegs, is the only person I can conceive of, sanguine enough to anticipate an evening's pleasure from a city sleigh-ride.

I can readily conceive that in the country, give a man a fast team, a light sleigh, a clear sky, a straight road, a pretty girl, plenty of snow, and a good tavern with a bright ball-room and capital music waiting at his journey's end, the frigid amusement may be made endurable—possibly, to a man enthusiastic enough to seek for pleasure with the thermometer at zero, even desirable.

But in New York, we can't get an unadulterated country sleigh-ride, any more than we can get genuine country milk—neither will bear importation. In both cases some unbargained-for dash of cold water interferes with the purity of the article, and nips in the bud our delusive anticipations.

The conditions necessary to a thorough-bred sleigh-ride can never be present in a great city. In the first place, the snow (an item of some importance) cannot even reach the earth unsullied; it is met in its quiet journey by some aspiring chimney, some impertinent roof, or ambitious spire, all dust-covered and smoke-begrimed, or by some other of the spontaneous nuisances indigenous to a city, and is robbed of its maiden purity, as its first welcome to the lower world—then, mixed with ashes, soot, and pulverulent nastiness of every sort—tainted with dainty perfumes of gas, garbage, markets and slaughter-houses, besides all the volatile filth of six hundred thousand perspiring bipeds (not mentioning hogs, horses, rats, dogs, and jackasses), it comes from upper air to us, expectant citylings—and even then we have to take it second-hand, for it is stopped in its airy transit by countless awnings, the tops of innumerable houses, stages, drays, and hackney-coaches, and the hats and outside apparel of the peripatetic multitude—from all which meddling mediums, it is transferred to the cold charity of the stony pavement, where the first instalment, in sorrow for its sullied purity, dissolves itself in discontented tears, and sulkily seeks, by some narrow down-hill track, its grave—the common sewer.

But a persevering snow-storm, which gives its whole attention to the work, sometimes succeeds in covering the streets of Gotham with a pepper-colored mixture, which we accept as snow.

When the air is cold, this peculiar substance cuts up into a kind of greyish sand, as much like real snow, as wild geese are like wooden legs—and when the weather is moist, it degenerates into a muddy, malicious mixture, in which the city flounders, until a drenching rain dilutes the mass into a coffee-colored flood, which sneaks into rivers through back lanes and dirty alleys, leaving the thoroughfares once more practicable. One week last winter eight inches of snow set our city people crazy, and turned Broadway into a horse purgatory. From Bloomingdale to the Battery, the street was filled with sleighs, cutters, pungs, jumpers and every variety of sled, all full of screeching, screaming men, women and children, in different stages of frigidity and voluntary discomfort, but all seeming, by their actions, to reiterate the cockney sentiment—"Wat's the hodds, long's you're 'appy?"

Every man who could hire or buy a transient interest in a string of bells and a horse, jackass or big dog, went in for an independent ride on his own hook—and those who could not compass this luxury, piled pell-mell into the stage sleighs, a hundred in a heap, each bound to have a sixpence-worth of slushy, slippery, horse locomotion.

At this crisis, Sandie proposed to me to join a company who were going to undertake an evening's pleasure, calculating to ride through the city, see the sights, go out of town to a ball, and dance till morning.

Agreed to go, put on my tightest boots, and got ready—time came, sleigh arrived, got in, received a promiscuous introduction to seventeen young ladies, by the light of a street lamp. Couldn't of course distinguish their faces so as to tell them apart, and so was continually calling Miss Jones, Miss Snifkins; Miss Loodle, Miss Vanderpants; and addressing Miss Faubob and Miss Wiggins by each other's names; which, as they were ready to scratch each other's eyes out for jealousy, and hadn't been on speaking terms for a year and a half, made the matter decidedly pleasant.

Found a place for my feet among the miscellaneous pedal assortment at the bottom—sat down, held on with both hands, and prepared to enjoy myself. After a great deal of whipping of the spirited horses, and some curiously emphatic observations by the driver, we got under way. Driver (an enthusiastic Hibernian with one black eye) took the middle of the street, resolved to give the road to nothing—met a young gent in a cutter, *he* didn't turn out, *we* didn't turn out, collision ensued, young man got the worst, his hat was smashed, and his delicate person left in a snow-bank—his horse started, hit against a lamp-post, then ran away, distributing the ruins of the cutter all along the road, leaving a piece at every corner and telegraph pole, until there wasn't enough left in any one spot to make a rat-trap—finally dashing through the show window of a confectioner's shop and being brought to a stand-still by the shafts sticking in a soda fountain.

Met a charcoal cart, run against us and distributed a shower of pulverized nigritude over the company, to the great damage of the clean linen of the gentlemen, and the adornments generally of the ladies, especially those little white rosettes which they had tied on the backs of their heads, and dignified with the fabulous title of bonnets.

Met a stage sleigh, got jammed with us—and during the three minutes preceding our violent extrication, I had leisure to take particular notice of the inmates.

Now, even in ordinary times, any kind of an omnibus is a purely democratic institution, but an omnibus sleigh containing ordinarily, anywhere from fifty to a hundred and twenty people, is a most effectual leveller of aristocratic distinctions.

In this particular vehicle, a fashionably dressed Miss, had from necessity, taken her seat in the lap of a Bowery boy, who, in his anxiety to make her comfortable, had put one arm round her waist, and one hand into her muff.

An up-town merchant was carrying a washer-woman's baby, while a dandy, in patent leather boots, was holding her bundle of dirty linen.

A news-boy, stealing a ride, was smoking a Connecticut cigar, and puffing the smoke into the faces of the incongruous assembly.

A negro woman was sustaining her position on the edge of the slippery craft, by holding on with one arm round the neck of a clergyman in a blue cloak with a brass hook and eye at the neck, who had a basket of potatoes with a leg of mutton in it, which a sailor was using for a shield to protect him from the shower of snow balls, fired by the boys on the corner—naughty boys—one hit one of our ladies on the head, she made a very pretty faint, but was soon revived by a piece of ice which I slipped down her back—one blacked the driver's other eye, and a particularly and solidly unpleasant one, hit Sandie in the mouth and waked him up.

Began to be sensible of the pleasures of my situation—felt as if my boots were full of ice water, my nose a Croton water pipe, and my fingers carrot-shaped icicles. Each leg seemed a perpendicular iceberg my feet good sized snow-drifts, my head a frozen pumpkin, and the inside of me felt as if I had made my supper on a cast-iron garden-fence.

As, however, these peculiar but unpleasant sensations are inseparable from the sleigh-riding performances, I tried to warm myself by imagining volcanoes and conflagrations; and, indulging in a hope of hot brandy and water at my journey's end, endeavoured to bear my trials like a frozen martyr, as I was.

Got to the hotel at last, waiters rescued us and got us into the house, which was full of parties ahead of us. Burnt the skin off my throat trying to thaw my congealed digestive apparatus, by drinking brandy and water boiling hot; ladies imbibed hot gin sling all round "*ad libitum*," gentlemen ditto, and "*Da Capo.*"

Ready for a dance; got into the ball-room, which was so full already that each cotillon had only a space about as big as a pickle-tub—"balance four" and you stepped on somebody's heels and tore off the skirt of some lady's dress—"forward two" and you poked your nose into the whiskers of the gentleman opposite, and felt his neck-tie in your eye, and "promenade all" was the signal for an animated but irregular fancy dance upon the toes of the by-standers.

But this quadrille was voted by most of our ladies to be altogether too antiquated and energetic—the truth is, city dancing is no more like a country jig than a dead march is like a hornpipe—in the one case the ladies slide about with a die-away air, as if one lively step would annihilate their delicate frames; and in the other, they dance as if they were made of watch-springs and india rubber.

The only way to get an ordinary city girl really interested in a dance, is to have some moustachoed puppy put his arm round her waist, hug her close up to him, spin her round the room till her head swims.

But the dancing couldn't last for ever, and at length we had to prepare for the ride home.

Towards morning the music got tired, the leading violinist was fiddling on one string on the wrong side of the bridge, and the ophicleide man, unable from sheer exhaustion to convey his potables to his mouth, was pouring them into his instrument, which he had regaled with four mugs of ale and a brandy smash, and the little fifer, with his foot in the big end of the French horn, was wasting his precious breath in trying to coax a quick step out of a drum-stick, which he mistook for a flageolet.

Compelled to stop dancing. Ladies went to a private room and repaired their damaged wardrobe with pins and other extemporaneous contrivances, known of them alone. Gentlemen put on what hats and great-coats the preceding parties had left, paid the bill—woke up the driver, and all started for home.

Shower came on, making the ladies look like damaged kaleidoscopes, and taking the starch out of the gentlemen's collars—the gum out of their hats, and the color out of their whiskers.

Upset—females got scattered round loose (horses didn't run away, not a bit of it), one young lady had her foot in my overcoat pocket, and both hands clinched in my hair—got out of the snarl at last, and found that I had traps enough hanging to me to manufacture a small-sized new married couple—a set of false teeth in my fur glove—two pairs of patent moustaches, with the springs broken, in my hat-band, half a head of glossy, ringleted hair in my button-hole, a lace collar hanging to my pantaloons, and my boots full of puff combs.

Righted up at last, hurried over mile-stones, curb-stones, and pebble-stones, till we reached the city—took the young ladies home, and was immediately after arrested by a moist watchman for being a suspicious character, and only identified by my friends in the morning, just in time to keep my name out of the papers.

Am completely disgusted with sleigh-riding—the enjoyment is purely imaginary, and the expense not at all so. Excitement aint pleasure, any more than sawdust pudding is roast turkey—and then too, the girls are so different—girls here are such touch-me-not creatures, that no one understanding the nature of the animal would venture on a kiss, unless he wanted to get his mouth full of magnesia and carmine; fuss, feathers, furbelows and flummery, will never make a *woman* out of any of these, until a new saddle and pair of gilt spurs will transform a sucking-calf into a race-horse.

A modern belle stands no kind of a chance with a country beauty—pale cheeks and dingy complexions may be *alleviated* by chalk and vermillion; but artificial hues are always evanescent, nature alone paints *cheeks* in fast colors. Sitting up late and guzzling brandy punches wont put the same kind of crimson in the face that is placed there by getting up in the morning, feeding the chickens, chasing the pigs out of the garden, and drinking sweet milk for breakfast. And not only in looks do they differ, but they

> "have yet
> Some tasks to learn, some frailties to forget."

An affected giggle won't pass muster for a hearty laugh—superficial boarding-school "finishing" is not education, for bad spelling will show, though the pen be held by jewelled fingers—and bad French, bad Italian, and worse English, are miserable substitutes for conversation, though uttered by the fairest lips that ever lisped in fashionable drawl.

It is true that in the circle of my limited acquaintance I have the honor to number some ladies whose unaffected manners, natural grace, and true politeness place even my usual awkwardness at perfect ease, while their superior intelligence causes me to feel most deeply my extensive *non-acquirements*—but to every one of these I have met twenty who, although they could dance, sing, play the piano; paint on velvet, or work in worsted, flowers unknown in botany, and animals to which ordinary natural historians are strangers; couldn't write an intelligible English note, or read anything more difficult than easy words in twc syllables; and if told that wheat bread is made out of kidney potatoes wouldn't know the difference.

I repudiate all this tribe of diluted milk-and-water misses, and should I ever feel matrimonially inclined shall commission some country friend to choose me a wife who can darn stockings, and make pumpkin pies anyhow, and hoe and chop cord-wood, if in any case the subscriber shouldn't be able to meet current family expenses.

## XXII

### Cupid in Cold Weather.—Valentine's Day.

IN accordance with some heathen custom, the origin of which is unknown to moderns, a certain day is selected in the year, when people send hosts of anonymous letters to other people, generally supposed to be on the subject of love, but which are not unfrequently missives containing angry, malicious, or insulting allusions. This is a day to rejoice the hearts of the penny postmen, who always get their money before they give up the documents. This glorious day is, as most people are aware, the fourteenth of February—time when young ladies expect to receive sentimental poetry by the cord, done up in scented envelopes, written upon gilt-edged paper, and blazoned round with cupids, hearts, darts, bows and arrows, torches, flames, birds, flowers, and all the other paraphernalia of those before-folks-laughed-at-but-in-private-learned-by-heart epistles known as "Valentines."

A time when young gentlemen let off their excess of love by lack-a-daisical missives to their chosen fair; praising in anonymous verses their to-other-eyes-undiscoverable-but-to-their-vision-brilliantly-resplendent charms—poetizing red hair into "auburn ringlets,"—making skim-milk-colored eyes, "orbs, the hue of heaven's own blue,"—causing scraggy, freckled necks to become "fair and graceful as Juno's swans," and deifying squat, dumpy young ladies into "first-rate angels."

A time when innumerable people take unauthorised liberties with the name of a venerable Roman, long since defunct, laying themselves under all sorts of obligations, payable in friendship,—pledging any amount of love, and running up tremendous bills of affections, making no solid man responsible therefor, but only signing the all-over-christendom-once-a-year-universally-forged cognomen "Valentine."

Most of these communications are amatory, some sickish, some nauseating, some satirical, some caustic, some abusive; for it seems to be a time which many a man takes advantage of to revenge some fancied slight from scornful lady, by sending her one of those scandalous nuisances, misnamed "comic Valentines;" because he thinks there will be so many of the foul birds upon the wing that his own carrion fledgling cannot be traced to its filthy nest.

Bull Dogge, who is looking over my shoulder, remarks, that the man who would insult a lady, by sending an anonymous letter, would steal the pennies from a blind man, and then coax his dog away to sell to the butcher boys.

And Bull Dogge is right.

A time when the penny postman is looked for with more interest than if he bore the glad tidings so anxiously expected, "Sebastopol not taken,"—Laura Matilda in the parlor, to whom he brings but one, looks with envious eyes upon Biddy in the kitchen who gets two.

A time when men who haven't got a wife wish they had, and those who are provided with that article of questionable usefulness wish they had another; when maids wish for one husband, and matrons for half a dozen.

A time when nunneries and monasteries go into disrepute, and the accommodating doctrines of Mahomet, and the get-as-many-wives-as-you-can-support-and-keep-them-as-long-as-they-don't-fight principles of Mormonism, are regnant in the land.

And above all, a time when independent bachelors like the deponent, are beset with so many written laudations of the married state, by unknown females, that every single-blessed man in all the land wishes he could take a short nap and wake up with a good-looking wife and nine large-sized children.

On the morning of this traditional pairing-off day, the postman brought me seventeen letters, all unpaid, and all from "Valentine." Retired to my room—closed the curtains—lit the gas—placed before me a mug of ale and two soda crackers, and proceeded to open and examine the documents.

No. 1 was sealed with beeswax and stamped with a thimble; and from its brown complexion, I should think it had fallen into the dishwater, and been dried with a hot flatiron. I couldn't read it very well—there wasn't any capitals—the g's and y's had tails with as many turns as a corkscrew, the p's bore a strong resemblance to inky hair pins, the h's resembled miniature plum trees; every f looked like a fish-pole, and every z like a frog's foot, and the signature I should judge had been made by the ink bottle, which must have been taken suddenly seasick, and have used the paper as a substitute for the wash-bowl.

All I could understand of it was "my penn is poor, my inck is pail, my (something) for yew shal never" do something else, I couldn't make out what.

No. 2 was in a lace envelope—cucumber-colored paper, and was perfumed with something that smelt like humble-bees; handwriting very delicately illegible, proving that it came from a lady—spelling very bad, showing that it came from a *fashionable* lady—poetry very unfamiliar, commencing "come rest in this" the next word looked like "boots," but that didn't seem to make sense—concluded it must be "barn-yard" as it went on to say "though the herd have fled from thee, thy home is still here." Couldn't make out whether she was in earnest and wanted me to come and see her, or was only trying to insinuate that I was a stray calf, and had better go home to my bovine parent.

(Bull Dogge says he wonders the ladies take such pains to render their correspondence unreadable—the up-strokes being just visible to the naked eye, and the down-strokes no heavier than a mosquito's leg—and why there is such a universal tendency to make little fat o's and a's just on the line, so that they look like glass beads strung on a horse-hair—and why they *will* persist in making their chirography generally so uncertain and undecided that a page of ordinary feminine handwriting looks like a sheet of paper covered with a half finished web, made by 'prentice spiders, and condemned as awkwardly clumsy by the journeymen spinners.

Will somebody answer Bull Dogge?

I soon threw aside No. 2 in disgust, and went on to the others—most of them pictured off with hymeneal designs; plethoric cupids with apostolic necks—flowers the like of which never grew anywhere—birds, intended for doves, supposed to be "billing and cooing," but which, in reality, more resembled a couple of wooden decoy ducks fastened together by the heads with a tenpenny nail—a heart stuck through with an arrow, reminding me of a mud turtle on a fish spear—little boy with a feather duster (supposed to represent Hymen with his torch,) standing by a dry-goods box with a marking brush sticking out at the top of it, (put by courtesy for an altar with a flame on it,) going through some kind of a performance with a young couple (supposed to be lovers intent on wedlock,) who appeared as if they had done something they were ashamed of, and deserved to be spanked and put in the trundle-bed —besides vines and wreaths, bows, arrows, babies, and other articles, the necessity of which to human happiness I have ever been at a loss to discover.

Some were complimentary and some abusive—one was from the bar-keeper and hinted at egg-nogg, insinuating that it wasn't paid for—and one I know was from Sandie, for it accused me of taking more than half the bed-clothes on cold nights. But I couldn't find out who wrote the good ones, and couldn't lick anybody for writing the bad ones, as the boys all denied it; and as they cost me three cents each, I've regretted ever since that I didn't sell them to the corner grocery man to wrap round sausages, and invest the money in a flannel nightcap.

## XXIII.

### The Kentucky Tavern.

THE State of Michigan having been the place of my preparation for College, and the Michigan University the scene of my brilliant though premature graduation, I was not wholly unacquainted with occidental geography. As I entered the Institution just mentioned, broke the rules, was tried, convicted, sentenced, punished, fined, suspended, and expelled in an unprecedented short space of time, no one was more fully prepared than I to admit that "this is a great country."

I was somewhat familiar with the entire country known as "out west;" had rode over it, walked over it, and been shot through it by steam; had stopped at all sorts of public-houses from the stylish hotel where you can get your liquor in glass tumblers, have stairs to get to your room with, and can repose on a bedstead, to the unostentatious tavern where the whiskey is served out in a tin dipper, and you have to climb into the garret by a ladder, and sleep on a bundle of straw, under the populous protection of a horse-blanket. But I never so thoroughly understood the discomforts of living at a hotel, as when on one occasion I strayed into the state of Kentucky, the land of good horses, poor jackasses, glorious corn-bread, and lazy darkies, and stopped at the best house of entertainment I could discover.

Having been thoroughly cooked by the broiling sun, which had unremittingly paid me his ardent devotions during the whole day—having been alternately melted and blistered—having had my skin peeled by the sun like a wet shirt from a little boy's back—having made a perfect aqueduct of myself for twelve hours in the fruitless attempt to keep cool, and having swallowed so much dust that I had a large sand-bar in my stomach, I sat down to write in as enviable a state of mind as can perhaps be imagined. I soon found that this was one of those stranger-traps into which unwary travellers are decoyed, and made to pay enormous prices for being rendered supremely unhappy—a place where *comfort* is mercilessly sacrificed to *show*—where the furniture is too nice to use, the landlord of too much consequential importance to treat people decently, and where there are so many dishes on the table that there is not room for anything to eat—where the waiters run in multitudinous directions at the tap of the bell, and seem to occupy most of their time stepping on each other's heels, and spilling soup into the laps of the ladies. Every one of these woolly-headed nuisances expects to be handsomely feed before he will condescend to pay the slightest attention to a guest, and a stranger must disburse an avalanche of "bits," "pics," and "levys," before he can get even a plate of cold victuals.

My experience at the house of entertainment at present under consideration is somewhat as follows:

I endure the inconveniences of the day with what philosophy I may, and retire, to "sleep, perchance." During the night I endeavor to bear without complaining the savage onslaught of ferocious fleas, the odoriferous attacks of bloodthirsty bed-bugs, and the insatiable and impetuous assaults of musically murderous mosquitoes, and eventually fall into a troubled doze, in which, like a modern Macbeth, who is doomed to "sleep no more," I tumble about until I am roused by the infernal clang of that most diabolical of all human contrivances—a gong, a dire invention of the enemy, a metallic triumph of the adversary, compounded of copper, and hammered upon with an "overgrown" drumstick, by a perspiring darkey who does not "waste his sweetness in the desert air" (more's the pity). After an abortive attempt to wash my face in what is truly *living* water, with a piece of marbleized soap, and hastily drying it upon three inches of towel with a ragged edge and iron rust in the corners, I proceed to dress.

Button off my shirt neck, which, being a matter of course, does not affect my equanimity half as much as finding that one of the sleeves is torn nearly across, and is only connected with the main body by a narrow isthmus of seam, which is momentarily growing "small by degrees and beautifully less."

Begin to grow impatient; second gong for breakfast; everything on but boots—open the door and find the porter has brought the wrong ones—he always does—ring the bell indignantly and sulkily wait (breakfast disappearing the meanwhile), until the blundering darkey explores his subterranean dominions and eventually returns with the missing articles.

Breakfast at last; waiter sets before me a mass of bones, sinews, and tendons, which he denominates *chicken*, and then brings me something which he calls *steak*, although but for the timely information I should have supposed it gutta-percha. Pours out a lukewarm muddy mixture supposed to have been originally coffee, which I sweeten with niggery brown sugar, and swallow at a gulp, ignoring the milk pitcher entirely on account of the variety of bugs which have found a "watery grave" therein; bread hard and greasy, butter oily and full of little ditches where the flies have meandered, knife with an edge like a saw, and fork with a revolving handle, table cloth splotchy, eggs hard as pebbles; rest of bill of fare consists of salt ham, red flannel sausages, hash with hairs in it, dip-toast made with sour milk, burned biscuit, peppery codfish, cold potatoes, mutton chops all bones, and mackerel with head, fins, and tail complete. Stay my stomach with half a glass of equivocal looking water, and exit.

Go to the office and order my room regulated immediately; go up in an hour and find two inches of dust over everything, my portfolios untied, books open at the wrong place, tooth-brush out and wet, and several long red hairs in my comb. Considerate, cleanly chambermaid!

Sit down on my carpet-bag and reflect—resolve to go back to Michigan.

Pack trunks, pay landlord, fee porter, hurry to the cars, tumble baggage on board, only too happy if by the diabolical ingenuity of the baggage-man it does not get put off at the wrong station. So ends my experience of the "Uncle Tom" State, which is probably the only place in the world where they hitch two jackasses before a dray, and get a big nigger with a red shirt on, up behind to drive 'em tandem.

# XXIV.

## The River Darkies.

TO a person not accustomed to the unaccountable antics and characteristic monkeyshines of the sable heroes of the corn fields, sugar plantations, flat-boats, and steamboat "'tween decks" of the lower river, a continual fund of amusement is afforded by their fantastic sayings and doings. On the Kentucky river I first observed some of their curious performances—the boats on this stream differ from any others in the world—the one on which I obtained my experience was peculiarly peculiar, and I find my impressions of the craft and the company recorded as follows :—

*Steamboat Blue Wing.*—Which said boat is very much the shape of a Michigan country-made sausage, and is built with a hinge in the middle to go around the sharp bends in the river, and is manned by two captains, four mates, sixteen darkies, two stewards, a

The River Darkies.

small boy, a big dog, an opossum, two pair of grey squirrels, one clock, and a cream-colored chamber-maid.

Fog so thick you couldn't run a locomotive through it without a snow-plough; night so dark the clerk has two men on each side of him with pitch-pine torches, to enable him to see his spectacles (he wears spectacles); pilot so drunk the boys have painted his face with charcoal and coke berries, till he looks like a rag carpet in the last stages of dilapidation; and he is fast asleep, with his legs (pardon me, but —legs), tied to the capstan, his whiskers full of coal-dust and cinders, and the black end of the poker in his mouth.

Boat fast aground, with her symmetrical nose six feet deep in Kentucky mud; there she complacently lies, waiting for the mail boat to come along and pull her out. Passengers elegantly disposed in various stages of don't-care-a-cent-itiveness, and the subscriber, taking advantage of the temporary sobriety of the clerk, and his consequent attendance in the after-cabin to play poker with the mates, embraces the opportunity to write. The silence is of brief duration, for I am interrupted by a grand oratorio by the nigger firemen, much to my delight and edification. It runs somewhat as follows:—

(Grand opening chorus) "A-hoo—a-hoo—hoo-oooo—a-hooo—a-hoo—a-hooo—a-hoooo-oo!"

The dashes in the following represent the passages where the superfluity of the harmony prevented the proper appreciation of the poetry.

"Gwin down de ribber—a-hoo-a-O!
Good-bye—nebber come back——debbil——beans ——Grey-haired injun——Ya-a—a—aaaa—Ya-a-a-a-a-a-a-a——
Ga—!" (leader of orchestra) "dirty shirt massa, got de whisky bottle in his hat, dis poor ole boy nebber git none——
A-hoo—a-hooo—a-hooooo!" (ending in an indescribable howl).
(Pensive darkey on the coal heap)—"Miss Serefiny good-bye—farewell; nebber git no more red pantaloonses from Miss Serefiny—Oho—Ahooo —Ahooo-O!"

(Extemporaneous voluntary by an original nigger with two turkey feathers in his hat, and his hair tied up with yellow strings)—
"Corn cake—'lasses on it—vaphuns—" (meaning waffles) "big ones honey on 'em—Ya-a-a-a-a-a."

(Stern rebuke by leader)—"Shut up your mouf, you 'leven hundred dollar nigger."

(Leader improvises as follows) "Hard work—no matter—git to hebben bym-bye—don't mind—go it boots—linen hangs out behind—" (here having achieved a rhyme, he indulges in a frantic hornpipe.) "My true lub—feather in him boots—yaller gal got another sweetheart—A-hoo—Ahoooooo!—Ahooooo-oo-O O O O!!!!!!——Hoe cake done—nigger can't git any—ole hoss in de parlor playing de pianny—You-a-a-a—Ga-Ga-Ga." Captain here interferes and orders the orchestra to wood up—and so interrupts the concert.

Have got over on the Indiana side, principal difference to be noticed in the inhabitants is in the hogs; on the Kentucky side they are big, fat, and as broad as they are long; on this side they are shaped like a North river steamboat, long and lean.

I just saw two of 'em sharpen their noses on the pavement, and engage in mortal combat; one rushed at his neighbor, struck him between the eyes, split him from end to end; cart came along, run over the two halves, cut them into hams and shoulders in a jiffy—*requiescat in many pieces.* This is decidedly a rich country; the staple productions are big hogs, ragged niggers, and the best horses in the United States. The people live principally on bread made of corn; whisky ditto; and hog prepared in various barbarous ways. They give away whisky and sell cold water. The darkies are mostly slaves; they nail horseshoes over their doors to keep away the witches, indulge in parti-colored hats in the most superlative degree of dilapidation, go barefooted, and have large apertures "in puppes pantalooni." It is a perfect treat to watch their entertaining performances. At the hotel the allowance is fourteen niggers to each guest, and as each one seems to be possessed of the peculiar idea that his province is to do nothing at all, with as many flourishes as possible, the confusion that follows is far from being devoid of entertainment.

They never bring you anything you call for; if you ask for chicken, you will probably get corned beef and cabbage; if you want roast beef, they will assuredly bring you apple dumplings; ask for sweet potatoes, and you'll get fried eggs; send for corn bread, and you're safe to obtain boiled pork; ring the bell for a boot-jack, and you'll get a hand-sled. And when you want to retire at night, instead of providing you with a pair of slippers and a candle, the chances are ten to one the attendant sable angel will give you a red flannel shirt, a shot-gun, a flask of whisky, three boiled eggs, and a pair of smoothing irons.

There is, however, one redeeming feature about the darkies, they won't live in the same country with Irishmen. They can live with hogs, have half a dozen shoats at the dinner-table, a litter of pigs in the family bed, but they can't abide Irish.

The slaves are, as may be imagined, of various colors, ranging from the hue of the beautiful yellow envelope of the Post Office Department, to that of the blackest ink that ever indites a superscription thereon. The theory of "woman's rights" is in practical operation among them; the men cook, set the table, clean up the dishes, do the washing, and spank the babies, while their blacker halves hoe corn, chop wood, go to market, and "run wid de masheen."

Have great fruit in this country; apples big as pumpkins; not very large pumpkins, small-sized pumpkins, diminutive pumpkins, infantile pumpkins, just emerged from blossomhood, and ere they have assumed that golden overcoat which maketh their maturer friends so glorious to the view. And pumpkin pies, manufactured by the sable god of the kitchen; pies enormous to behold; wherein after they are ready to be devoured you might wade up to your knees in that noble compound which filleth the interior thereof, and maketh the pie savory and nectarean; in fact, pies celestial, whereof writers in all ages have discoursed eloquently.

To return to the principal topic—the darkies—they are all built after the same model; hand like a shoulder of mutton, teeth white as milk, foot of suitable dimensions for a railroad bridge, and mouth big enough for the depot; have all got six toes on each foot, skull like an oak plank, yellow eyes, and nose like a split pear.

## XXV.

### The Thespian Wigwam.

IT naturally required some considerable time to recover from the tremendous effect produced upon my nervous system, by witnessing the unequalled acting of the "American Tragedian;" so that several weeks elapsed before I felt again disposed to visit a theatre.

At length, however, I began to feel a longing for the green curtain again; and feeling time hang heavy on my hands from the fact that I had an entire evening at my own disposal, I held a great consultation with my inseparable friends, on the most feasible and agreeable method of sacrificing the great horological enemy.

After mature deliberation, we resolved to visit the lately established, "truly gorgeous temple of the 'muses,'" and witness the redemption of one of the pledges of the Directors, who had promised us the restoration of the legitimate classic drama. We believed that there we should find "true artistic taste, displayed in the adornment and decoration of the building," and that we should see "sterling plays acted by performers of the highest merit; where every attention would be paid to propriety and elegance of costume, and splendor and magnificence of stage appointments."

We took a stage and navigated up Broadway until we came opposite Bond street, to the place where a big canvas sign marks the entrance to the "*Grand Thespian Wigwam, and Head Quarters of Modern Orpheus.*"

Through a wedge-shaped green-baize door—down a crooked pair of stairs—under an overhanging arch —and we stood in the parquette.

Took a front seat, and immediately had occasion to commend the economy of the managers in not lighting the gas in the upper boxes—then proceeded to admire in detail the many beauties of this superb edifice, which, at first glance, reminded me of an overgrown steamboat cabin.

Looked for a long time at the indefinite Indian over the stage, trying to fix the gender to my satisfaction, and decide whether it is a squaw or an individual of masculinity—hard to tell, for it has the face, form, and anatomical developments of the former, and the position and hunting implements of the latter—I concluded that it must be an original Woman's Rights female, who, in the lack of breeches, had taken possession of the "traps" of her copper-colored lord and master, and, getting tired of the unusual playthings, had lain down to take a snooze.

Admired the easy and graceful drapery painted on the "drop," which looks as if it was whittled out of a pine shingle—took a perplexed view of the assorted landscape depicted thereon—endeavored to reconcile the Turkish ruins with the Swiss mountains, or the Gothic castle with the Arab slaves—wanted to harmonize the camels and other tropical quadrupeds on the right, with the frozen mill-pond on the left—couldn't understand why the man on the other side of the same, among the distant mountains, should be so much larger than the individual close to the shore, who is supposed to be nearer by several miles.

Tried to make out what the man in a turban is doing with his legs crossed under him, on a raft, but gave it up—admired exceedingly the two rows of private boxes, which looked like windows in a martin-house, but could not perceive the propriety of having them supported by plaster of paris ladies, without any arms, and their bodies covered up in patent metallic burial-cases. (I was informed that the artist calls them *Carỳatides.*)

Was impressed with the admirable proportions of the stage; a hundred and eleven feet wide, by four feet ten inches deep—reminded me forcibly of an empty seidlitz-powder box, turned up edgeways—censured the indelicacy of the managers in permitting the immodest little cupids, who tacitly perform on the impossible lutes and fiddles, to appear before so refined an audience, "all in their bare"—(my friend says the drapery was "omitted by particular request.")

Was much chagrined about a mistake I made concerning a picture on one of the proscenium flats, which I mistook for a Kentucky backwoods girl, with a bowie-knife in one hand and a glass of corn-whiskey in the other; but I was told that it represents the tragic muse, with the dagger and poison bowl.

Resolved not to be deceived about the match picture on the other side, and after an attentive scrutiny, I determined that it is either a female rag-picker with a scoop-shovel, or a Virginia wench with a hoe-cake in her hand; and I made up my mind that any one disposed to heathenism might safely worship the same, and transgress no scriptural command, for it certainly is a likeness of "nothing in the heavens above, the earth beneath, or the waters under the earth." Many other barbaric attempts at ornamentation claimed my attention, and would have received particular notice, had I not perceived by the stir in front of the stage that the performance was about to commence.

The multitudinous orchestra came out in a crowd —the big fiddle man took the emerald epidermis from off his high-shouldered instrument, and after a half hour preparatory tuning, and forty-one pages of excruciating overture, the little bell *didn't* ring (they never ring a bell at this aristocratic establishment—it smacks of the kitchen), but with a creaking of pulleys, a trampling of feet, a rattling of ropes, and a noise like a full-grown thunderstorm, the curtain went up.

Magnificent forest scene—two blue-looking trees on one side—a green baize carpet to represent grass —blue calico borders over head to suggest sky—a bower so low the hero thrice knocked his hat off going under to see his "lady love," and a mossy bank in one corner, made of canvass, stretched over a basswood plank, and painted mud color.

Audience all silent, waiting the coming of the "Evening Star," the lovelorn heroine of the piece—at length she comes—with a hop, step, and a jump, she blushingly alights in the middle of the stage—applause—she teeters—cheering—she teeters lower yet—prolonged clapping of hands—boquet hits her on the head; she picks it up and teeters lower still—a dozen or so more fall at her feet, or are scattered indiscriminately over the fiddlers and the boys in the front row—somebody throws a laurel wreath—she again teeters to the very earth, so low that I think she will have to sit flat down and pick herself up by degrees at her leisure, but she ultimately comes up all right.

Melodramatic villain comes on with a black dress, and a blacker scowl on his intellectual visage—has some hard words with the heroine—she calls him a "cowardly wretch," a "vile *thing*," defies him to his teeth, tells him to do his worst, and finishes in an exhausted mutter, in which I could only distinguish disconnected words, such as "poison," "vengeance," "heaven," "justice," "blood," "true-love," and "death."

Despairing lover appears in the background, remarkable principally for his spangled dress and dirty tights, at sight of whom the defiant maid immediately changes her tune, and prays powerful villain to spare her beloved Adolphus—powerful villain scowls blacker, and turns up his lip—heroine gets more distracted than before—scowly villain won't relent—suffering young lady piles on the agony, and implores him "to save my father from a dungeon, and take this wretched hand."

Powerful villain evidently going to do it, when heroic lover comes down on a run, throws one arm around his lady-love, draws his sword with the other, strikes a grand attitude, and makes a terrific face at powerful villain, who disappears incontinently—lover drops his bloodthirsty weapon, slaps his hand on his breast, and the interesting pair pokes their head over each other's shoulders, and embrace in the orthodox stage fashion.

Scene closes.

Magnificent chamber, furnished with a square-legged table, two chairs, and carpets whose shortcomings are distinctly visible to the naked eye—triumphal march, long dose of trumpet, administered in a flourish—supposed to portend the advent of royalty.

Enter procession of badly scared " supes," with cork whiskers, wooden spears, pasteboard helmets, tin shields resplendent with Dutch metal, and sandals of ingenious construction and variety—they march in in single file, treading on each other's heels, keeping step with the majestic regularity of a crowd of frightened sheep escaping from a pursuing bull-dog, and form a line which looks like a rainbow with a broken back.

King swaggers in, looking very wild—distracted heroine enters all in tears, her hair down her back, her sleeves rolled up, (evidently being convinced that "*Jerdon* is a hard road,") and her general appearance expressive of great agony of mind.

She makes a tearing speech to the king, during which she rolls up her eyes, throws her arms about, wrings her hands, pitches about in a certain and unreliable manner, like a galvanized frog—sinks on her knees, rumples her hair, yells, cries, whispers, screams, squirms, begs, entreats, dances, wriggles, shakes her fist at powerful villain—stretches forth her hand to heaven—throws her train around as if she was cracking a coach whip—slides about like a small boy on skates, and at length, when she has exerted herself till she is hoarse, she faints into the arms of heroic lover, who stands convenient; her body from the waist up being in a deep swoon, while her locomotive apparatus retains its usual action, and walks off without assistance, although the inanimate part of her is borne away in the careful arms of the enamored swain in the dirty tights.

Several scenes follow, in all of which the heroic lover, the dark villain, and the despairing maiden, figure conspicuously, and the scenic resources of this magnificent establishment are displayed to the utmost advantage—the omnipresent square-legged table being equal to any emergency—being an ornament of elegant proportions in the palace, then an appropriate fixture in the lowly cot of the "poor but honest parents" of heroic lovers.

It is used by the King to sign a death-warrant on, and is then transferred to the kitchen, where it makes a convenient platform upon which the low-comedy servant dances a hornpipe—it then reappears in the country-house of a powerful villain, who uses it by night for a bedstead—and it then makes its final appearance in the King's private library, prior to its eventual resurrection in the farce, where bar-maid has it covered witl pewter beer-mugs and platters of cold victuals.

And the same two ubiquitous chairs go through every gradation of fortune, turn up in all sorts of unexpected places, are always forthcoming when we least expect to see them—are chairs of state or humble stools, as occasion may require—are put to all sorts of uses—appear in varied unexpected capacities, and finally, when we think their Protean transformations are at last exhausted, they re-appear, covered with flannel ermine and Turkey red calico, doing duty as thrones for the King and Queen, and we are expected to honor them accordingly.

The end draws nigh—brigands begin to appear in every other scene—dark lanterns, long swords, and broad cloaks are in the ascendant.

Terrible thunder-storm prevails—the dashing rain is imitated as closely as dried peas and No. 1 shot can be expected to do it—the pendant sheet iron does its duty nobly, and the home-made thunder is a first-rate article. The plot thickens, so does the weather—heroic young lover is in a peck of troubles—has a clandestine moonlight, midnight meeting with injured damsel, and they resolve to kill themselves and take the chances of something "turning up" in another world.

Comic servant eats whole mince pies, drinks innumerable bottles of wine, and devours countless legs of mutton and plum-puddings at a sitting.

Villain is triumphant—blood and murder seem to be victorious over innocence and virtue—when suddenly "a change comes o'er the spirit of their dreams."

Heroic lover resolves not to die, but to distinguish himself—fights a single-handed combat with seven robbers—stabs three, kicks one into a mill-pond, and throws the rest over a precipice—distressed maid is pursued by bandit chief—is rescued by heroic lover, who catches her in his arms and jumps with her through a trap-door over a picket fence.

Hero is unexpectedly discovered to be a Prince, which fact is made known to the world by his old nurse, who comes from some unknown region, and whose word everybody seems to set down as gospel.

Despairing lady proves to be a Princess—King summons all hands to appear before him—heroic lover plucks up courage, runs at big villain with his sword—fight, with all the usual stamps by the combatants, and appropriate music by the orchestra.

Big villain is stabbed—falls with his head close to the wing—prompter slaps red paint in his left eye—looks very bloody—acts very malicious—spits at heroic lover—squirms about a good deal—kicks his boots off—soils his stockings, and after a prolonged spasmodic flourish with both legs, his wig comes off, he subsides into an extensive calm, and dies all over the stage.

Everybody is reconciled to everybody else. King comes down from his throne to join the hands of the loving pair, and immediately abdicates in favor of persevering lover—people all satisfied—young husband kisses his bride, leaving part of his painted moustache on her forehead, and she, in return, wipes the Venetian red from her cheeks upon his white satin scarf—Grand Tableau—triumph of virtue (painted young man and woman) over vice—(big dead rascal). Everybody cries "hooray"—curtain goes down.

The appreciating audience congratulate themselves on having done their part to encourage and sustain the "Modern Classic Drama."

Had I not been informed by the advertisement of the "Grand Thespian Wigwam," that this was a specimen of a sterling "legitimate Classic Drama," I should have supposed it to be a blood and thunder graft of another stock transplanted here for the delectation of "upper-tendom"—from the rustic shades of the unmentionable Bowery.

Since my visit to this Modern Temple of the Drama, it has been converted into a Circus, and the Home of Tragedy has been changed into a "Ring" for the Exhibition of Summersets and Sawdust.

## XXVI.

### Theatricals Again—A Night at the Bowery.

NOT satisfied with having seen the place of amusement referred to in the last chapter, I also desired to go over to the twenty-five cent side of the town, and behold the splendors of their dramatic world. Accordingly, I've been to the Bowery Theatre—the realm of orange-peel and peanuts—the legitimate home of the unadulterated, undiluted sanguinary drama—the school of juvenile Jack-Sheppardism, where adolescent "shoulder hitters" and politicians in future take their first lessons in rowdyism.

Where the seeds of evil are often first planted in the rough bosom of the uncared-for boy, and, developed by the atmosphere of this moral hot-house, soon blossom into crime.

Where, by perverted dramatic skill, wickedness is clothed in the robes of romance and pseudo-heroism so enticingly as to captivate the young imagination, and many a mistaught youth goes hence into the world with the firm belief that to rival Dick Turpin or Sixteen-String Jack is the climax of earthly honor.

A place where they announce a grand "benefit" five nights in the week, for the purpose of cutting off the free-list, on which occasions the performance lasts till the afternoon of the next day.

Where the newsboys congregate to see the play, and stimulate, with their discriminating plaudits, the "star" of the evening.

For this is the spawning-ground of theatrical luminaries unheard-of in other spheres; men who having so far succeeded in extravagant buffoonery, or in that peculiar kind of serious playing which may be termed mad-dog tragedy, as to win the favor of this audience, forthwith claim celestial honors, and set up as "stars."

And a star benefit-night at this establishment is a treat; the beneficiary feasts the whole company after the performance, and they hurry up their work as fast as possible so as to begin their jollification at the nearest tavern; they have a preliminary good time behind the scenes with such viands and potables as admit of hurried consumption.

So that while the curtain is down, Lady Macbeth and the witches may be seen together drinking strong-beer, and devouring crackers and cheese; and after Macbeth has murdered Duncan, and Macduff has finished Macbeth, they all three take a "whisky skin," and agree to go fishing next Sunday.

The "Stranger" plays a pathetic scene, rushes from the stage in a passion of tears, and is discovered the next minute eating ham sandwiches and drinking Scotch ale out of the bottle—or Hamlet, after his suicidal soliloquy, steps off, and, as the curtain descends upon the act, dances a hornpipe with a ballet-girl, while the Ghost whistles the tune and beats time with an oyster-knife.

But the Bowery audiences are, in their own fashion, critical, and will have everything, before the curtain, done to suit their taste.

An actor must do his utmost, and make things ring again; and wo be to him who dares, in a ferocious struggle, a bloody combat, or a violent death, to abate one single yell, to leave out one bitter curse, or omit the tithe of a customary contortion. He will surely rue his presumption, for many a combatant has been forced to renew an easily won broadsword combat, adding fiercer blows, and harder stamps—and many a performer who has died too comfortably, and too much at his ease to suit his exacting audience, has been obliged to do it all over again, with the addition of extra jerks, writhings, flounderings, and high-pressure spasms, until he has "died the death" set down for him.

An actress, to be popular at this theatre, must be willing to play any part, from Lady Macbeth to Betsey Baker—sing a song, dance a jig, swallow a sword, ride a bare-backed horse, fight with guns, lances, pistols, broadswords, and single-sticks—walk the tight-rope, balance a ladder on her nose, stand on her head, and even throw a back-summerset. She must upon occasion play male parts, wear pantaloons, smoke cigars, swear, swagger, and drink raw-whiskey without making faces.

The refined taste which approbates these qualifications is also displayed in the selection of dramas suitable for their display. Shakspeare, as a general thing, is too slow. Richard III. might be endured, if they would bring him a horse when he calls for it, and let him fight Richmond and his army single-handed, and finally shoot himself with a revolver, rather than give up beat.

Macbeth could only expect an enthusiastic welcome, if al. the characters were omitted but the three witches and the ghost of Banquo ; but usually nothing but the most slaughterous tragedies and melo-dramas of the most mysterious and sanguinary stamp, give satisfaction.

A tragedy hero is a milk-sop, unless he rescues some forlorn maiden from an impregnable castle, carries her down a forty-foot ladder in his arms, holds her with one hand, while with the other he annihilates a score or so of pursuers, by picking up one by the heels, and with him knocking out the brains of all the rest, then springs upon his horse, leaps him over a precipice, rushes him up a mountain, and finally makes his escape with his prize amid a tempest of bullets, Congreve rockets, Greek fire and bomb-shells.

Thus it may be supposed that no ordinary materials will furnish stock for a successful Bowery play. Probabilities, or even improbable possibilities, are too tame. Even a single ghost to enter in a glare of blue light, with his throat cut, and a bloody dagger in his breast, and clanking a dragging chain, would be too common-place.

When the boys are in the chivalric vein, and disposed to relish a hero, to content them he must be able, in defence of distressed maidens, (the Bowery boys are ragged knights-errant in their way, and greatly compassionate forlorn damsels,) to circumvent and destroy a small-sized army, and eat the captain for luncheon.

If they are in a murderous mood, nothing less than a full-grown battle, with a big list of killed and wounded, will satisfy their thirst for blood; and if they fancy a touch of the ghastly, nothing will do but new-made graves, coffins, corpses, gibbering ghosts, and grinning skeletons.

I went by the old, damaged, "spout-shop" the other day—saw a big bill for the evening, and stopped to read—magnificent entertainment—to commence with a five-act tragedy, in which the hero is pursued to the top of a high mountain, and after slaying multitudes of enemies, he is swallowed up by an earthquake, mountain and all, just in time to save his life.

Professor Somebody was to go from the floor to the ceiling on a tight rope, having an anvil tied to each foot, and a barrel of salt in his teeth—then the interesting and bloody drama, "the Red Revenging Ruffian Robber, or Bold Blueblazo of the Bloody

Bradawl"—after which, a solo on the violin, half a dozen comic songs, three fancy dances, and a recitation of the "Sailor Boy's Dream," with a real hammock to "spring from," three farces, and a comic opera—then Bullhead's Bugle Band would give a concert, assisted by the Ethiopian Minstrel Doves—then an amateur would dance the Shanghae Rigadoon on a barrel-head—after which Madame Jumpli Theo. Skratch would display her agility by leaping through a balloon over a pyramid, composed of a hose truck, two beer barrels, and a mountain of green fire.

Numberless other things were promised, in the shape of Firemen's addresses, songs, legerdemain, acrobatic exercises, ventriloquism, &c., the whole to conclude with an original Extravaganza, in which the whole company would appear.

I paid my money, and got inside. A great many straight-up-and-down red-faced ladies were in the boxes, with cotton gloves on, and bonnets so small you couldn't tell they had any at all unless you went behind and took a rear view—and a multitude of men who chewed a great deal of tobacco, and sat with their hats on; a policeman stood in front of the stage, and made a great deal of noise with a cane, and constituted himself a nuisance generally.

The Pit, the dominion of the newsboys, was full of these young gentlemen, in their shirt-sleeves, with boots too big, and caps perched on the extreme supporting point of the head (the New York newsboy always puts his cap on the back of his neck, and pulls all his hair over his eyes), who were remarkably familiar and easy in their manners, and all had bobtailed appellations; no boy had a whole name any more than a whole suit of clothes; nothing more than Bob or Bill, with an adjective prefixed, which transformed it into "Cross-eyed Bob," or "Stub-legged Bill."

They enjoyed the performances much; they cheered the tragedy man when he howled like a mad-bull, and hammered his stomach with both hands; applauded the injured maiden when she told the "villain," "another step, and she would lay him a corpse at her feet," at the same time showing a dagger about as big as a darning-needle, and also, when in despair at being deserted by the fellow in the yellow boots, in a spangled night-gown, she poisoned herself with something out of a junk-bottle, and expired in satisfactory convulsions.

They threw apples at the man who walked up the rope, and tossed peanuts on the stage when the girl with the foggy dress was going to dance; they called the actors by their names as they came on the stage, audibly criticising their dress and manner, the performers often joining in the conversation—one instant talking heroic poetry to some personage of the scene, and the next inquiring of Jake, in the pit, how he would trade his bull-terrier for a fighting-cock and a pair of pistols.

I stayed all night and watched the fun—began to get hungry—audience all tired, and actors asleep on the stage from sheer exhaustion—the noisy policeman was leaning against the orchestra railing fast asleep—the boys had blacked his face with a burnt cork, filled his boots full of peanut-shells, and cut a hole in his hat to put a candle in; those boys who were awake were pulling the boots off the sleepy ones, and putting them into the bass drum through a hole which they had punched with a crutch.

On the stage the Emperor was sleeping on his throne, with his mouth open like a fly-trap—the "injured lady" had sunk flat down upon the floor—a robber lay each side—she was using the "villain" as a pillow, and had her feet tangled in the hair of the "Amber Witch," who was sleeping near.

I noticed the short-skirted dancing-girl reposing

upon a pile of "property" apple-dumplings, and the prompter was stretched on the top of a canvas volcano, with the bell-rope in his hand, and his hair full of resin from the "lightning-box."

Had enough theatre for once—went straight home, got a late breakfast, and went to bed just as the clock struck three-quarters past ten.

Doesticks in the Lodge of the K. N.'s.

## XXVII.

### Mysterious Secrets of the K. N's.—A Midnight Initiation.—Philander Fooled.

HAVING of late heard a great deal about a mysterious individual known as "Sam," I felt a strong desire to become more intimately acquainted with a person of so much importance. Expressing a desire to that effect one day in presence of a young friend who wore a set of gold stars on the front entrance of his shirt, and had a star breast-pin, with the number 67 on it, he informed me that he knew the residence of the omnipresent Samuel, and that, if I desired, he would put me in the way to gain the like knowledge.

I snapped at his offer, and he told me to be at the foot of the Grand street Liberty-pole at 2 o'clock in the morning, singing "Hail Columbia," the "Star Spangled Banner," and "Yankee Doodle," in alternate verses. That I must have a copy of the constitution in my coat pocket, that at intervals I was to sing out "Yankee," and that when an individual replied "Doodle" I was to take him by the arm and go whither he should lead.

Bull Dogge accompanied me and we followed our directions to a dot.

After standing in the cold till our jaws rattled like a dice-box, a person in a long cloak appeared. I whispered "Yankee," Shanghae-like he responded "Doodle," and arm-in-arm we started.

We went through a long series of lanes, alleys, stair-cases, up ladders, and through cellars, and at last came to an out-of-the-way room which we could only enter by climbing up a two-inch rope and crawling on our hands and knees on the roof about half a block, then letting ourselves down through the garret-window.

Immediately on our entering the room, I was seized by several men, blind-folded by having a red liberty-cap pulled over my eyes, and gagged with the butt-end of a Yankee flag-staff.

Soon a gruff voice pronounced the mystic words, "off with the night-cap." The cap was hastily removed, when the same voice continued, "let there be light."

It was undoubtedly the intention to have a brilliant illumination immediately follow this command, that the opening scenes of the initiation might be grand and impressive.

The solemnity of the thing was, however, sadly interfered with by having bad lucifer matches which would not take fire, notwithstanding the active exertions and "curses not loud" but still audible, of the member who was striving to ignite the same by rubbing them on the sole of his boot, in which endeavor he broke them all in two, and split his finger nails on the pegs in his heels.

After some delay, however, "there *was* light," and then I discovered my situation.

In a long room, a wooden statue of the Goddess of Liberty, at one end; a picture of La Fayette, with a cocked hat on, at the other; and a man in a pulpit in the middle, dressed up to represent Washington, in a revolutionary uniform, with his hair powdered, and a sword in his hand. As I approached him he gave me a goblin wink with his left eye, shook his fist at me solemnly, and began to question me concerning my nativity. Told him I was a full born Yankee, that the sight of an Englishman makes me mad and fighty, that I wanted to kick every Frenchman who comes in my path, and to trip up every Dutchman, and that even the most distant glimpse of an Irishman makes me sick at the stomach.

Said he thought I'd do, and told the rest to put me through the sprouts.

They wrapped me in an American flag, made me kneel down before the white oak goddess of Liberty and solemnly swear hatred to the Pope, the abolitionists, and the king of England, death and destruction to all foreigners, and eternal fidelity to "Sam;" that I never would employ Irishmen, never work for an Irishman, never have my washing done by an Irishwoman, or my shirts made of Irish linen, and that when I said the prayer in the book for all the world, I should make a special reservation of the Irish, and insert a petition that in the general resurrection they be overlooked "by particular desire."

At this juncture Bull Dogge fainted away, and was brought to by the High Lord Noodle throwing dirty water in his face, and treading on his corns.

I was then made to stand upon my feet, hold up my right hand, and take a terrible swear to the effect that I would never reveal the grand principle of the order; which is to get trusted at the Irish groceries, and use their liquor as long as credit holds out, in order to drink up all the Irish whiskey, and get it out of the country; the supposition being, that when the liquor is gone and the potato rot has done its worst, the Irish will all perish for want of nourishment.

Should any survive this annihilation of their national and necessary food, it is proposed to organize a company of volunteer Native Know Nothing Thugs, who are to circulate through the country and make an end of the rest, and at the same time sack all the nunneries, burn all the Popish churches, and finish up all the Foreign Catholics.

I was promised by the Ineffable Noodle, that if I did my duty well I should have the pleasure of choking a dozen or two priests, burning a couple of churches, and running away with the prettiest nun I could pick out.

Instructions were then given me how to work my way into a lodge of unadulterated Know Nothings.

Every member gives the pass-word, at the door (which is "Whiskey," and "Lager Bier," on alter nate months), walks to the centre of the room, faces the Most Illustrious Ineffable, puts the thumb of his left hand on the tip of his nose, grinds an imaginary hand organ with the other, at the same time looking cross-eyed at the nonsensical numskull.

Each member is bound to bring a bottle of Irish whiskey to every meeting, and drink it all before he goes, in order to prove his devotion to the cause, and his determination to expunge the foreign element from the liquid comforts of the country.

The recognition of members in the street is as follows:—One rolls his chew of tobacco into the upper story of his left cheek, at the same time motioning with his thumb over his shoulder towards the nearest grocery; if the other nods his head and starts towards the rum-shop on a run, the question of fraternity is decided, and they know each other as members of the K. N. brotherhood.

Since my initiation I have striven to live up to the principles of the order, and have got trusted for so much Irish liquor that I have kept all my friends dead drunk for a month, and have three times had to bail Bull Dogge out of the station-house, whither he had been taken for being inebriated in the street, and giving the K. N. signs to the M. P., and trying to pull his star off, insisting that an Irishman has no right to wear the badge of the order.

The intention is to elect the next President, when

there is to be an immediate end made of all foreigners; they will drown the Dutchmen in Lager Bier, pelt the Irish to death with potatoes, and pen up all the Frenchmen in second-hand flat-boats, and send them over Niagara Falls.

I was expelled from the order for eating Dutch "Sauerkrout" with an oyster stew, and I am now in danger of losing my life, as I hear that the Ineffable Noodle is on the look-out for me, having two revolvers and a bowie-knife in his bosom; a Congreve rocket in his hat; a six inch bomb in each pocket; a large jack-knife in his pantaloons; and a Mexican lasso round his waist.

P. S. I have just discovered that I have been hoaxed—that the lodge into which I was admitted is not the genuine article, but a spurious society who take in members under false pretences, by making them believe that this is the society of "Sam."

The truth is, however, that "Sam" lives in different quarters, and has a different set of people about him; and if I can gain admission to a lodge of the pure-bred K. N's., I may then be able to tell something more of the hidden mysteries of this popular individual.

## XXVIII.

### A Diabolical Conspiracy—A Shanghae Infernal Machine.

I HAVE been the recipient of an unexpected favor. I have been gratified by a bipedal compliment, and have here publicly to acknowledge the receipt of a rare bird of unexampled dimensions—a Shanghae Rooster, with double teeth, which has been presented to me by our friend, the "Young 'Un."

When I desire to speak of the various beauties of this feathered pledge of friendship, language can't come to time. His legs rival the Grand-street liberty-pole, in length, size, and symmetry—in fact, he exhibits rather a strong tendency to run to legs; his plumage is variegated and generally shaggy, and his disposition courageous; he has an eye like a hen hawk, a tail like the butt-end of a feather-duster, and a voice like a rhinoceros with the whooping cough;

he is perfect in every point; to combine in a single expression, the elegance and euphony of the ancient Latin tongue, and the expressive intensity of the more modern Bowery idiom, he is literally "gallus."

He is a present from Burnham, Professor No. 1 of Henology, and such a proficient in universal humbug that he ranks only second to the Bridgeport Fejee Prince—Burnham, who made one fortune by selling "pure bred" Shanghae stock, and another by showing up the tricks of the trade, and the mysteries of Roosterdom, in a blue covered book, with gilt edges, and who has now left the hen trade, only keeping on hand a few chicks, of warranted *pure* blood, which he prescribes at high prices to any anxious individuals who haven't yet had the "hen fever"—(a popular epidemic, price $1, can be caught at any book store).

How they ever got my bird from Boston to New York, I am uncertain; but I have the authority of the engineer for stating that they switched the locomotive off on a side track, and made him draw the passenger train.

Got him home; for fear he should stray away in the night, anchored him in the barn yard to a brick smoke-house, with a chain cable. Was waked up in the morning by a sound like an army of tom-cats, in league with a legion of amateur musical bull-frogs —listened—heard it again—thought my time had come—covered my head up with the bed-clothes—was soon startled by the sudden disappearance of the same—looked up and saw that Mr. Shanghae had poked his head in at the third story window, and was pulling the covers off me with a vengeance; he made a grab at my leg, but I hit him with a boot-jack, and succeeded in impressing him with the idea that he was trespassing; kept out of his reach during the day, and watched him from a distance; he has to get down on his knees to eat, inasmuch as his neck isn't more than half as long as his legs. But I admire his beauties, though I can't conceive what he's made for; and I can bear ample testimony to the excellence of his appetite. On the whole, I am delighted, and the donor has my sincere thanks.

ONE WEEK LATER.

What kind of a fellow is Burnham?

Is he a malicious, unscrupulous conspirator?

What can I have done to provoke his ire?

This voracious animal which he has given me is eating me out of house and home; my means are limited, my salary is small, corn is expensive, and at the present rate one of us must starve; he has eaten every thing I have given him, and (the poor brute being tortured by growing hunger) he has at last actually *devoured his own toes.*

Two small pigs and a litter of kittens have also mysteriously disappeared; one of the children last night was attacked by the monster and barely escaped with his life, but left his Sunday breeches in the unappeasable maw of the *pure* bred biped, who has twice been observed to cast longing eyes upon the Irish kitchen girl—the cannibalic feathered Know Nothing.

Like the eastern prince, who, when he wants to ruin a man, makes him a present of an elephant, which court etiquette will allow him neither to give away, sell, or kill, and which he must keep and allow to devour his patrimony; so the vengeful Burnham, for some unmentioned injury which I have done him, has sent me this rapacious villain, who eats as if he was the result of a cross between the Anaconda and the Ostrich. I must get some one to kill him, or coax him into the rural districts, where they might use him for a breaking-up team, or some two or three counties club to keep him as a curiosity.

### ONE HOUR LATER.

Our stable boy, half an hour ago, found the bird suffering an indigestion (consequent upon eating a bushel and a half of corn with the cobs in, a pyramid of oyster shells, and a barrel of guano), and boldly attacking him with a revolver and broad-axe, has succeeded, after a prolonged struggle, in making an end of him. I ask B. if his fiendish and diabolical malice is sated.

### THE VERY LATEST.

I have for sale half a ton of feathers, which would make capital bean poles, a side of tanned Rooster hide, and two Shanghae hams.

## XXIX.

### An Evening with the Spiritualists—Rampant Ghostology.

AFTER the election excitement was over with, all ordinary means of amusement seemed "stale, flat, and unprofitable." I no longer took any interest in Theatres, Balls, or Darkey Minstrelism—and even a fire at midnight failed to rouse me from my bed, unless it was in the next block, visible from my window without getting up, and I could hear Hose 71 pitching into Engine 83 on the next corner.

A near relative of the illustrious Damphool, who believed in the Spiritual performances, persuaded me to visit, with him and my inseparable friends, the habitation of a "Medium" who retailed communications from the other spheres at twenty-five cents an interview.

Being sated with the ordinary common-place things of every-day life, and having heard a great deal about the mysterious communications telegraphed to this, our ignorant sphere, by wise and benignant spirits of bliss, through the dignified medium of old chairs, wash-stands and card-tables, we three (who had met again) determined to put ourselves in communication with the next world, to find out, if possible, our chances of a favorable reception when business or pleasure calls us in that direction.

Up Broadway, till we came to an illuminated three-cornered transparency, (which made Bull Dogge smack his lips and say "oysters,") which informed us that within, a large assortment of spirits of every description were constantly in attendance, ready to answer inquiries, or to run on errands in the spirit world, and bring the ghosts of anybody's defunct relations or friends to that classic spot, for conversational purposes, all for the moderate charge before mentioned.

Damphool, who had been there before, said that these "delicate Ariels" were the spirits of departed newsboys, who are thrown out of their legitimate business, and strive to get an honest living by doing these eighteen-penny jobs.

Entered the room with *be*coming gravity, and *over*-

coming awe. Two old foozles in white neckcloths and no collars, a returned Californian in an Indian blanket, two peaked-nosed old maids, a good-looking widow, with a little boy, our own sacred trio, and the "medium," composed the whole of the assembled multitude.

The "medium" aforesaid, was a vinegar-complexioned woman, with a very ruby nose, mouth the exact shape of the sound-hole to a violin, who wore green spectacles, and robes of equivocal purity.

The furniture consisted of several chairs, a mirror, no carpet, a small stand, a large dining table, and in one corner of the room a bedstead, washstand, and bookcase, with writing desk on top. After some remarks by the medium, we formed the magic circle, by sitting close together, and putting our hands on the table. Bull Dogge, who, despite the Maine law, had a bottle in his pocket, took a big drink before he laid his ponderous fists by the side of the others.

After a short length of time the table began to shake its ricketty legs, to flap its leaves after the manner of wings, and to utter ominous squeaks from its crazy old joints.

Pretty soon "knock" under Damphool's hand; he trembled, and turned pale, but on the whole, stood his ground like a man. Knock, *knock* in *my* immediate vicinity—looked under the table, but couldn't see any body—knock, *knock*, KNOCK, KNOCK, directly under Bull Dogge's elbow. He, frightened, jumped from his seat, and prepared to run, but, sensible to the last, he took a drink, felt better—reverently took off his hat, said "d—n it"—and resumed his seat.

Knocking became general—medium said the spirits were ready to answer questions—asked if any spirit would talk to me.

Yes.

Come along, I remarked—noisy spirit announced its advent by a series of knocks, which would have done honor to a dozen penny postmen "rolled into one."

Asked who it was—ghost of my uncle—(never had an uncle)—inquired if he was happy—tolerably.

What are you about?

Principal occupations are, hunting wild bees, catching cat-fish, chopping pine lumber, and making hickory whip stocks.

How's your wife?

*Sober*, just at present.

Do you have good liquor up there?

*Yes* (very emphatically).

What is your comparative situation?

I am in the second sphere; hope soon to get promoted into the third, where they only work six hours a day, and have apple dumplings every day for dinner—good-bye—wife wants me to come and spank the baby.

One of the old foozles now wanted to talk spirit—was gratified by the remains of his maternal grandmother, who hammered out in a series of forcible raps, the gratifying intelligence, that she was very well contented, and spent the most of her time drinking green tea and singing Yankee Doodle.

Damphool now took courage, and sung out for his father to come and talk to him—(when the old gentleman was alive, he was "one of 'em)"—on demand, the father came—interesting conversation—old man in trouble—lost all his money betting on a horse race, and had just pawned his coat and a spare shirt to get money to set himself up in business again, as a pop-corn merchant.

(Damphool sunk down exhausted, and borrowed the brandy bottle.)

Disconsolate widow got a communication from her husband that he is a great deal happier now than formerly—don't want to come back to her—no thank you—would rather not.

Old maid inquires if husbands are plenty—to her great joy is informed that the prospect is good.

Little boy asks if when he gets into the other world he can have a long tail coat—mother tells him to shut up—small boy whimpers, and says that he always *has* worn a short jacket, and he expects when he gets to Heaven, he'll be a bob-tail Angel.

Damphool's attention to the bottle has re-assured his spirits (he is easily affected by brandy—one glass makes him want to treat all his friends—when he has two bumpers in him he owns a great deal of real estate, and glass No. 3 makes him rich enough to buy the Custom-House), and he now ventures another inquiry of his relative, who shuts him up, by telling him as soon as he gets sober enough to tell Maiden Lane from a light-house, to go home and go to bed.

Went at it myself; inquired all sorts of things from all kinds of spirits, "black spirits and white, red spirits and grey." Result as follows.

By means of thumps, knocks, raps, and spiritual kicks, I learned that Sampson and Hercules have gone into partnership in the millinery business. Julias Cæsar is peddling apples and molasses candy.

Tom Paine and Jack Sheppard keep a billiard table. Noah is running a canal boat. Xerxes and Othello are driving opposition stages. George III. has set up a caravan, and is waiting impatiently for Kossuth and Barnum to come and go halves. Dow, Junior, is boss of a Methodist camp meeting.—Napoleon spends most of his time playing penny "ante" with the three Graces. Benedict Arnold has opened a Lager-bier saloon, and left a vacancy for S. A. Douglas (white man).

John Bunyan is a clown in a circus. John Calvin, Dr. Johnson, Syksey, Plutarch, Rob Roy, Davy Jones, Gen. Jackson, and Damphool's grandfather were about establishing a travelling theatre; having borrowed the capital (two per cent. a month)—they open with "How to pay the Rent;" Dr. Johnson in a fancy dance; to conclude with "The Widow's Victim," the principal part by Mr. Pickwick.

Joe Smith has bought out the devil, and is going to convert Tophet into a Mormon Paradise.

Shakspeare has progressed in his new play as far as the fourth act, where he has got the hero seven miles and a half up in a balloon, while the disconsolate heroine is hanging by her hair to a limb over a precipice; question is, how the heroic lover shall get down and rescue his lady-love before her hair breaks, or her head pulls off.

Spirits now began to come without invitation, like Paddies to a wake.

Soul of an alderman called for clam soup and bread and butter.

Ghost of a newsboy sung out for the Evening Post.

All that was left of a Bowery fireman, wanted to know if Forty had got her butt fixed and a new inch and a half nozzle.

Ghost of Marmion wanted a dish of soft crabs, and called out, after the old fashion, to charge it to Stanley.

Medium had by this time lost all control over her ghostly company.

Spirits of waiters, soldiers, tailors (Damphool trembled), babies, saloon-keepers, dancers, actors, widows, circus-riders, in fact all varieties of obstreperous sprites, began to play the devil with things generally.

The dining table jumped up, turned two somersets, and landed with one leg in the widow's lap, one in Damphool's mouth, and the other two on the toes of the sanctimonious-looking individuals opposite.

The washstand exhibited strong symptoms of a desire to dance the Jenny Lind polka on Bull-Dogge's head.

The book-case beat time with extraordinary vigor, and made faces at the company generally.

Our walking canes and umbrellas promenaded round the room in couples, without the slightest regard to corns or other pedal vegetables; while the bedstead in the corner was extemporizing a comic song, with a vigorous accompaniment on the soap-dish, the wash-dish, and other bed-room furniture.

Bull Dogge here made a rush for the door, and dashed wildly down Broadway, pursued, as he avers to this day, by the spirit of an Irishman, with a pickaxe, a handsaw, and a ghostly wheelbarrow.

Concluding I had seen enough, I took Damphool and B. D——'s bottle (empty, or he would never have left it), and went home, satisfied that "there are more things in heaven and earth than are dreamed of," except by lying "*mediums*," so called; who too lazy to work, and too cowardly to get an honorable living by stealing, adopt this method to sponge their bread and butter out of those, whom God in his mysterious wisdom has seen fit to send on earth weak enough to believe their idiotic ravings.

## XXX.

### Special Express from Dog Paradise—A Canine Ghost.

I REGRET the strong language used in the preceding chapter, for since it was penned I have become a firm believer in ghosts, "spheres," saltatory furniture, and the other doctrines of professed Spiritualists.

It is a solemn truth that I, Q. K. Philander Doesticks, P. B., although neither a doctor, clergyman, nor Judge of the Supreme Court, have received a visit from the spirits. The secrets of the other world have been partially revealed to me.

I have had a glimpse of horse-heaven—a very fair view of the very blissful residence of pigs and poultry, and been vouchsafed a key-hole peep at the paradise of Spiritual Jackassdom.

I have discovered that Esop is a reliable historian,

and I find that in a future world the power and liberty of quadrupedal speech will be restored in all its pristine euphony and elegance. Listen, wonder, and believe!

Some time since, I had a beloved and beautiful bull-terrier—(not the Bull-Dogge alluded to in other epistles,) he was perfect in every point—his hair stuck out in multitudinous directions—his snarl was of the crossest—his teeth of the sharpest, and his ordinary behavior exhibited a general and impartial hatred of mankind. He was a canine Ishmael, for every man's hand was against him. His cognomen savored of the satanic. I called him Pluto.

He mysteriously disappeared—an offered reward of seven dollars and a half failed to restore him to my fireside. I tearfully gave him up, and mourned sincerely. I suspected the dog-killers, and wept for him as for one gone "to that bourne from which" bull-terriers don't come back.

Last evening I was aroused from a thoughtful contemplation of my nightcap (liquid and hot, with nutmeg,) by the unusual and remarkable conduct of a pet tom-cat, who deliberately climbed upon my lap, and, in a voice intelligible, if not absolutely musical, spoke to me—positively spoke to me!—he informed me that various spirits were present who desired to hold communication with me.

Having recovered somewhat from my momentary astonishment, I sung out to fire away.

No sooner said than done—the services of the feline "medium" were instantly dispensed with, and there suddenly appeared to my bewildered sight the unmistakable form of my lamented Pluto.

I was astonished, and so I said, but I could not be deluded—it was my "real, old, original, genuine" Pluto. I knew his warning growl—I recognized the friendly wag of his tail—I could have sworn to each particular hair.

He addressed me in a voice trembling with emotion—he narrated the full history of his untimely decease—told of his *se*duction by a tempting mutton chop, and consequent *ab*duction by the remorseless thief—his vain and ineffectual struggles to escape—related his incarceration in an unseaworthy canal-boat, with a hundred other unfortunates—described their embarkation and departure for a foreign market—the terrific collision which ensued when about four miles and a half from port, when the canal-boat was met by a mudscow which was recklessly running with great velocity in a thick fog, the entire force of her propelling apparatus (one-horse power) being brought into requisition to attain a frightful speed—he dwelt upon the terrors of the scene—the dastardly desertion of the crew, (a mulatto woman and two coffee-colored boys,) who took to the boat, (a bass-wood "dugout,") and escaped, leaving the helpless passengers to their awful fate. He told the agonies he endured when submerged in the raging flood—his attempt to save himself upon an empty cheese-tub. How he was crowded off by a frightened spaniel pup—the last excruciating, agonizing pain of the final struggle, and his subsequent entrance to the canine spirit world. He whispered, in a mysterious tone, that he had just come from a sixpenny eating-house, where he had witnessed the final disappearance of his mortal remains through the jaws of a confiding drayman who had asked for a mutton pie.

The whole history was related with an appearance of earnestness and sincerity which left not a doubt of its truth; and the entire narrative was couched in such elegant language that I strongly suspected that Pluto had read the report of those accommodating spirits who had imparted such reliable information concerning the untimely loss of the lamented steamship "Arctic," to a distinguished, and formerly-supposed-sensible-and-sane, Judge of the Superior Court for the Empire State. And, like those unfortunate ghosts, these, too, came to reveal to mortal ears the story of their sufferings and death.

For my beloved animal was not alone: with him appeared the disembodied ghosts of all the crowd who perished with him.

Pluto informed me that they were in such a disturbed state of mind that they did not know much yet—most of them were not permanently billeted—but that he himself, on account of his superior sagacity, had been already assigned his sphere and situation. He volunteered to show me some of the celebrities.

With a majestic motion he moved his pathetic tail, and forth they came in grand procession, the "Happy Family" being headed by old Mother Hubbard's dog and Dick Whittington's cat, in neighborly proximity.

From a hurried inspection I was enabled to gather the following items: The Trojan horse was suffering from indigestion; Coleridge's "mastiff bitch" has just become the happy mother of thirteen lovely cherubs, and is "as well as can be expected;" "the rat that eat the malt that lay in the house that

Jack built" says the Maine Law would have spared him that early indiscretion; Balaam's ass had his jaw tied up with the toothache; Rozinante was in good racing condition; St. George's dragon looks much more amiable than I should have supposed; Bucephalus and Old Whitey had been fighting a pitched battle, and are on short allowance of oats for insubordination; the Fee Jee mermaid said she had got tired of her Caudal appendage, and desired me to ask Barnum, if her tail must be continued.

Jonah's whale, some time since, swallowed the Nassau-st. four-cent man, but gave him up, like a second Jonah, and he is now on his old "stamping-ground" again. In the distance, I perceived John Gilpin's horse, and the bull that was unceremoniously displaced from a well known architectural elevation, and was informed that Nebuchadnezzar, who had not yet lost his fondness for greens, sometimes shares their pasture with them.

The Black Swan, the Swan of Avon, and the patriotic geese whose intellectual cackling saved Imperial Rome, were enjoying themselves in catching tadpoles in a duck-pond.

Walter Scott's dog Maida, Beth Gelert, Launce's dog, old dog Tray, and the other "Tray, Blanche, and Sweet-heart," were discussing canine politics over a beef-bone.

The Sea Serpent appeared, but was so dimly visible that I could only judge him to be about the average length.

Edgar A. Poe's Raven and Barnaby Rudge's Grip had just been detected stealing corn from a quail-trap, and hiding it in an empty powder-horn.

Many other birds of note were pointed out, and their situation and prospects explained by the oblig-ing Pluto.

And, even as one of our most learned, wise and illustrious rulers, and his brother Rapperites, have demonstrated that the spirits of the departed are busied in employments similar to their earthly ones, so did my reliable Pluto state similar facts concerning the honorable company of beasts, birds, and reptiles. His discourse ran much as follows:

"Know, men of earth, that shadowy horses still throng your streets, harnessed to intangible drays, and to incorporeal express wagons, and still tailfully drag innumerable three-cent stages; they still live in your stables, graze in your pastures, and drink at your pumps; drivers, malignant, though unseen, still lash their unreal sides with cutting whips, until they become overcome with ire, and viciously kick over their spectral traces; defunct racers still haunt the scenes of their former triumphs, skim with feet unshod round the inside track, and scornfully turn up their goblin noses at the fastest earthly time on record; transparent donkeys wag complacently their celestial ears, and brush off airy flies with unsubstantial tails.

"Swine, full grown, although unseen, proud as in life, ferociously prowl about your streets, seeking what they may devour, and expressing with inaudible grunts their Paradisiac satisfaction; bodiless pigs squeal under formless gates; dogs still follow, with unheard tread, their dreamy masters, wagging their placid phantom tails, or searching through their shaggy hides, with savage teeth, for spiritual fleas.

"Polecats, invisible, still haunt your barns, searching for airy chickens, finding ghostly eggs in unheard of nests—then stealing and giving odor in your cellars; apparitions of departed cats hunt pulseless mice, and in your parlors, phantom kittens chase their goblin tails. Henceforth, let every man take heed, lest, in pulling off his boots, he kick his dear departed Carlo; and let every maiden lady bestow herself in her favorite rocking-chair, in awe and perturbation, lest the cushion be already occupied by defunct Tabby and her spectral litter."

When my darling Pluto had spoken thus, the company began to disappear. A mist seemed gradually to envelope all, and one by one they faded from my mortal vision, and soon all save Pluto had vanished from my sight. He only remained, to give me one last assurance that the creed of the well known Indian mentioned by Mr. Pope, is true—who firmly believes that in the happy hunting ground hereafter,

"His faithful dog shall bear him company."

## XXXI.

### 'Lection Day.—"Paddy" versus "Sam."

EVERYBODY knows that Election day anywhere creates an unusual excitement; but it is in the large cities where partisan feeling runs the highest, where strongest and strangest influences are brought into requisition to influence the election of favorite candidates; where the people are made to act as blind confederates in a skilful scheme of party trickery and political legerdemain, which places one man into office, and defeats the expectations of another, whom they fully expected to see invested with the imaginary robes of municipal power. So dexterously are the cups and balls shifted by the party leaders, and so cunningly is the pack shuffled, that the rank and file of the different cliques can't tell where the "little joker" is, or who holds the trump card, for an hour together.

The first election witnessed by the undersigned,

was one of unusual interest, principally on account of the intense antagonism of the foreign and the know-nothing elements of party, and the tremendous exertions of "*Sam*" to overthrow his great rivals, "*Paddy*" and "*Hans.*"

Early in the morning of the day I was in the street, to see whatever fun might turn up—found it filled with big placards, posters, music, notices, split-tickets, rum-bullies, banners, bonfires, and lager-bier—saw a great many flags with appropriate devices, noticed one in particular; the whiskey faction had it; coat of arms as follows:

Within the American shield, two lager-bier casks supporting a rum-bottle rampant, Irishman azure, flat-on-his-back-ant, sustained by a wheelbarrow couchant—sinister eye sable in-base, demijohn between two small decanters—in the distance, policeman pendant, from a lamp-post standant—motto, "Coming events cast their shadows before: Let the M. P.'s beware." On the obverse, ticket for city officers, and opposed an American quarter dollar—motto, "Exchange no Bribery." "Faugh na Ballagh." "Go in and win."

As has ever been the case, from the time of the first institution of public elections, it rained as if it was raining on a bet—went to the polls, wanted to vote, wasn't particular who for, if he only had the biggest flags and the most bullies: was a little puzzled after all how to do it; had read all the political prints to find out the best man, but to judge from what the newspapers say concerning the different candidates, the various factions in this city entertain peculiar ideas about the requisites necessary to qualify a man to fill a public station.

Not an individual is ever nominated for any office, who is not eulogized by some of the public journals, as a drunkard, liar, swindler, incendiary, assassin, or public robber.

Assuming from the wonderful unanimity of the papers on this subject, that these amiable qualities constitute the fitness of the nominees for places of honor, trust, or profit, I have endeavored to analyze the gradations of criminal merit, and discover exactly how big a rascal a man must be to qualify himself for any given office. The result of my investigation is as follows:—

No one is eligible to the office of Mayor of the city, unless he has forged a draft, and got the money on it; and, on at least two separate occasions, set fire to his house, to get the insurance.

Candidates for Aldermen qualify themselves by carrying a revolver, getting beastly drunk, and stabbing a policeman or two before they can get sober.

A Common Councilman must drink with the Short Boys, give prizes to the Firemen's Target Excursion, carry a slung-shot in his pocket, and have a personal interest in a Peter Funk auction shop.

A police Justice must gamble a little, cheat a considerable, lie a good deal, and get drunk "clear through" every Saturday night; if he can read easy words, and write his name, it is generally no serious objection; but the Know Nothings will not permit even this accomplishment, on the plea that the science of letters is of foreign origin.

A man who can pick pockets scientifically, will make a good constable.

Aspirants to minor offices are classified according to desert, but no one who has not at least committed petit larceny, is allowed a place on any regular ticket.

As to offices of more importance, I should say from what I can now judge, that no man can ever be elected Governor of the State, unless he is guilty of a successful burglary, complicated with a midnight murder.

The rival candidates in this present crisis, had called each other all the names, and accused each other of all the crimes imaginable, for the preceding six weeks.

Boggs had been denounced as the plunderer of orphans, and seducer of innocent maidens, and the pilferer of hard-earned coppers from the poor.

Noggs, according to his charitable opponents, was a pickpocket, a sheepstealer, a Peter Funk, and an Irishman.

The candidate set up by the Know Nothings, to claim votes on the plea of his being an immaculate American, was proved to be the child of a French father, and a Prussian mother, and to have been born in Calcutta—it was asserted that he commenced his education in the northern part of Ethiopia, continued it in Dublin, and finally graduated at Botany Bay.

Hoggs, who had once before held the office he was now striving for, it was asserted, had solemnly promised to pardon all the murderers, liberate all the burglars, reward all the assassins, and present all the shoulder hitters with an official certificate of good moral character, which should also testify to their valuable and highly commendable exertions in the public behalf.

Scroggs, too virtuous to be severely handled, was merely mentioned as having been formerly a swindler, and a member of the Common Council.

Got to the polls; man with a blue flag urged me to go for Boggs; man with a red flag said vote for Scroggs; man with a white flag with black letters sung out "Go for Hoggs"—little boy pulled my coat tails and whispered, "Vote for Noggs."

Man challenged my vote, took off my hat, held up my hand, and swore to all sorts of things, told how old I am, where I get my dinners, and what my washerwoman's name is; got mad and did a little extra swearing on my own account, which was not "down in the bill;" marched up in a grand procession of one, and poked my vote in the little hole.

The great excitement was on the liquor question; it was Noggs, and no liquor shops, or Boggs, and a few liquor shops, Scroggs, and plenty of liquor shops, or Hoggs, and every man his own liquor shop.

Voted for Hoggs, for I feel perfectly justified in

taking an occasional toddy, when all Wall street is perpetually "tight."

Noise on the corner, nigger boy playing big drum —candidates presented themselves to the sovereign people for inspection.

Know Nothing man on a native jackass, cap of liberty on his head, and his pantaloons made of the American flag, with the stripes running the wrong way.

Independent candidate, who wants the Irish vote and Dutch suffrages, entered, borne in a mortar hod, bare-footed, with a shillelagh in one hand, a whiskey bottle in the other, a Dutch pipe in his mouth, and a small barrel of beer strapped to his back.

Cold water man stood on a hydrant with the water turned on, and had his pockets full of icicles.

Whiskey man brought in drunk on a cart by admiring friends, who besought the crowd to do as he did, go it blind.

Special deputy, who wanted to be appointed policeman, was very active; he arrested an apple-woman, knocked down a cripple, kicked a little boy, looked the other way while his constituents were picking pockets, and took a little match girl up an alley and boxed her ears for presuming to show herself in the street without shoes and stockings,—motto on his hat, "*sic itur ad astra*," Go it or you'll never be a star.

Irish woman, with a big bag of potatoes on her head, came up to vote—she said Dennis was sick, (drunk) but as Mr. Hoggs had paid for his vote, she had brought it herself, in order that it might not be lost. She was, with difficulty, choked off by the heroic aspirant to the civic star.

Whiskey man began to fall behind; messenger sent to Randall's Island, and one to Blackwell's ditto, for aid.

Fresh caught Irishman came up—been but fifteen minutes off the ship "Pauper's Refuge," but was brought up by the bullies to vote for whiskey man —Know Nothing man challenged him—he swore he was twenty-seven years old, had always lived in this country—ten years in Maine—eleven in South Carolina—eight in Maryland, and the last nine years of his life he had spent in this city. Said he was a full-blooded American; that his father was a New Hampshire farmer, and his mother a Mohawk squaw; that they had separated three years before he was born, and had never seen each other since.

Inspector, who was a friend of whiskey man, received his ballot. (Paddy had slipped in two others with his left hand, while his right was on the book taking the oath.) His kind friends took him by turns into eighteen different wards, in every one of which he deposited a whiskey vote, and swore it in; after the polls were closed and he couldn't vote any more, they sent him to the station-house for being "drunk and disorderly."

Elated with their success in this instance, the B'hoys now brought up a newly imported Dutchman, who could only grin idiotically and say "Yaw."

Inspector asks—"Are you a voter?"

"Yaw."

"Are you twenty-one years old?"

"Yaw."

"Do you live in this city?"

"Yaw."

Here one of Noggs's friends culpably interposed, evidently with the desire of ridiculing the august proceedings, and asked:

"Have you got thirty-one wives?"—another man asked if he had his hat full of saur-krout—and a third was anxious to be informed if he could stand on his head and smoke a pipe, and balance a potash kettle on his heels; to all of which he placid y responded "Yaw."

Inspector hurried to the rescue, and put the test question:

"Do you vote for Hoggs?" and receiving the same complacent "Yaw," he took his vote, and shoved him aside.

All sorts of odd customers came up to deposit their ballots, but it is a remarkable fact that if they wanted to vote for Boggs, Scroggs, or Noggs, or, in fact, any one but Hoggs, they were sure to be crowded, shoved, and hustled, and generally left the room with bloody noses, and their ballots still in their hands.

Fun grew fast and furious; whiskey man ahead, but wanted tremendous majority; the pauper forces of Randall's Island, visiting the city for that occasion only, came up and voted.

This last trick is getting stale, and whoever is elected this time will probably have it denounced as a diabolical invention of the opposite faction, and have a sharp watch kept over these individuals until his own term of office runs out, and he is announced as a candidate for re-election; which circumstance will blind his eyes for a while unless his opponents bring them over to the other side, when he will turn state's evidence, and expose the whole trick to his constituents.

Almost time to close the polls, but the inspector kept the box open twenty minutes after sundown to receive the votes of sixteen promiscuous rascals, who had been habeas corpused from the Tombs, and who voted every man for Hoggs.

Polls closed; intense excitement; bonfires built; squibs, rockets, guns and Chinese crackers; liquor scarce, the candidates having cut off the supply as soon as the voting was over.

Crowd sat down in bar-rooms and engine-houses, and crowded about the secret rooms to get dispatches; about twelve o'clock they began to come: it was soon evident that Noggs was beaten, Boggs was distanced, and Scroggs was nowhere; it was Hoggs everywhere; Hoggs in the street; Hoggs in the tavern; Hoggs at the bonfires; Hoggs for ever; no one but Hoggs; triumphant Hoggs; victorious Hoggs; high-old Hoggs, the people's choice.

This morning Noggs's typographical organ announced the utter ruin, and speedy annihilation of the country, under the destructive rule of Hoggs; and it asserted that honor, honesty and truth had left the nation; patriotism and decency had deserted hand in hand, and that the outraged goddess of liberty had taken off her night-cap, pinned up her skirts, put on a pair of cowhide boots, and bidden eternal farewell to fallen, degenerate Columbia.

On the other hand, Hoggs' papers rejoiced over the defeat of the allied armies. Bade Noggs, Boggs and Scroggs an affectionate adieu, and consigned them to oblivion; and then rejoiced that they had chosen a ruler so capable as the glorious Hoggs, the proud, far-seeing, generous, liberal, independent Hoggs, who guaranties to the people their daily gin, and nightly riots. Hoggs, the magnanimous—Hoggs, who stands up to the popular creed—unlimited whiskey—Hoggs, who remains true to his alcoholic instincts—Hoggs, who battles for the people's rights —Hoggs, who has so nobly earned the title bestowed upon him by the lager-bier shops, whose liberty he has secured, and the whiskey dens whose morality he has vouched for—HOGGS, "defender of the Faith, and leader of the Faithful."

P. S. Hurrah for *Hoggs.*

P. S. Junior.—And unlimited whiskey.

# XXXII.

## Police Adventures.—Mayor Wood around.

HAVING made myself so exceedingly useful to the party in the last election, I thought it not improbable that the party might not be indisposed to make itself useful to me afterwards.—Was undecided what office to ask for, but thought I would like to be an M. P.

I have so long admired the public usefulness of those blue-uniformed men, chained to big brass stars (as if they were members of some locomotive K. N. Lodge), who stand on the corners, borrow the morning papers of the newsboys and munch gratuitous peanuts from the apple-women's stalls, that I, too, felt a desire to serve the city by wearing a broadcloth suit, carrying a lignum-vitæ club, and drawing my salary on pay-day.

I have often noticed the alacrity with which they pilot unprotected females across the street, boost them into stages, or land them, dry-shod, on the curb stone as the exigencies of the case may require—the ferocity with which they crack their whips at tardy omnibus drivers—the courage with which they attack the street-sweeping children, and small-sized apple-women, and the diligence with which they get the legs of their pantaloons dirty, endeavoring to keep the course of travel uninterrupted in the streets.

Having an innate love of courage and noble deeds, (my father was Captain in the artillery,) I could not but look with admiration upon the chivalrous manner in which four or five of them will undauntedly lay hold upon a single man, if *very* drunk—and the courageous valor they display in fearlessly knocking off his hat, intrepidly twisting their fingers in his neck-cloth, unshrinkingly stepping on his toes and kicking his shins, and stout-heartedly rapping his knuckles with their hard wood clubs.

Emulous to rival such doughty heroism, I made application for the situation of policeman, "Z., 785," which position had been vacated by the chief, in consequence of the late incumbent having got drunk at the corner grocery, and pawned his uniform and star to get money to bet on a rat-terrier.

There were thirty-six applicants of various nations, for the post—soon saw that Yankees stood no kind of a chance—so swore I was an Irishman, and proved my birth by carrying a hod of mortar to the top of a five story building without touching my hands—after that had more of a sight, but found I had a powerful rival in the person of a six foot Welshman, a rod and a half across the shoulders, with a fist like a pile-driver—both swore we were "dimmycrats."

They asked us what we had done to secure the election of the regular ticket.

Welshman said he had voted twice, built bonfires, carried flags, torn down the handbills of the opposite party, and that just before the time for voting was up, perceiving a crowd of our opponents about the polls, he had raised an alarm of fire and got an engine company to come tearing through the crowd and scatter them so that they couldn't get their votes in before the doors closed.

Now came my turn—told them I had got up six free fights, challenged fourteen whig voters, knocked the hats over the eyes of eight of them and changed their tickets in the confusion, thereby making them vote for Hoggs, when their bread and butter depended upon the election of Noggs.

Swore also that I had voted in eight different wards, (three times in the 46th by the aid of a red wig and a pair of false whiskers)—and also that I had associated with me in my operations, a genteel party of eleven Dutchmen, made them all swear in their votes at every place I did, and at three o'clock in the afternoon, when lager-bier had done its worst, and they were so far overcome with their patriotic exertions, that they couldn't hold their heads up, I locked them safely in a barn, so that the whigs might not find them, drown them with a sober hydrant stream, and put them through the same exercise all over again.

Told them I had finished the day by getting up a row in the office, breaking the inspector's spectacles with a brick, and slipping into the ballot-box sixty-three votes for Hoggs before he got the glass out of his eyes.

Welshman couldn't talk so fast, and so they decided that I was the best qualified, and had the strongest claims.

Got the appointment, had my uniform made, was presented with a star and a club, and entered upon the performance of my duties.

Was stationed at the corner of Maiden Lane and

Broadway, to keep the street clear—endeavored to do it—express-man's horse fell down—tried to get him up—ungrateful horse—very—turned over suddenly, threw me down—spoiled my pantaloons, and bit a long piece out of my coat collar.

Got him up at last, and while the driver was reloading his vehicle, tried to put on the gearing—never tried to harness a horse before, don't think I could do it well without practice.

Got the breeching over his eyes, the hames between his foreshoulders, buckled the belly-band round his ears, forgot the collar entirely, and hooked the traces to the fore-wheels—driver didn't seem to like my way of doing things, but at last he got every thing fixed right and passed along.

Alarm of fire—tried to keep the engines from running on the sidewalk—as a reward for trying to do my duty, got run over by two hose-carts, and a hook and ladder truck, and was knocked bodily into an ash-box by the foreman of engine 73.

Mighty torrent of opposing vehicles got jammed —stages, carts, coal-waggons, drays, hackney-coaches, two military companies with a brass-band, a four-horse hearse with a long funeral procession.

Every body very obstinate, wouldn't move—tried to disentangle them—got bewildered, made every thing worse—horses fell down, stages fell on top of them—mourners escaped with their lives—coffin didn't—hearse tipped over and pitched into a swill-cart—soldiers stuck their bayonets through the omnibus windows, ladies screamed, drivers yelled—got scared—didn't know what I was about, ordered everybody to go everywhere, put half the mourners into a Crystal Palace stage, and sent them up town, and the rest into a private coach, and sent them *down* town—got the coffin out of the swill-tub, and despatched it by express to the Hudson River Railroad.

Couldn't with all my exertions get the tangle unsnarled, and it was only eventually accomplished by the Captain of the Police Division, who came to my assistance, and made every thing all right in about two minutes and a half.

Was sent to a drinking saloon to take a couple of river thieves—found the place, arrested two suspicious-looking persons, got them to the Chief's office after a great deal of trouble, and then discovered that I had let the right men go, and secured only the bar-tender and one of the waiters.

Was sent with half a dozen others to capture a notorious burglar—tracked him to his house—the rest went inside to look for him, and left me to watch the garden wall to see that he didn't get out that way.

Saw a man getting over, rushed up to him, asked him who he was—said he was a stranger in the city, that the wind had blown his hat over the wall, and, having recovered it, he was just climbing back; gentlemanly-looking man—believed his story, helped him over, asked if I shouldn't brush his clothes, said he had an appointment and couldn't wait; let him go, and he disappeared round the corner just as the rest of my company came down stairs after an unsuccessful search for the burglar; asked if I'd seen anybody—told them about it. and Sergeant informed me that I'd been helping the very man to escape whom they were trying to take.

Believed him for I now discovered that he had stolen my week's salary from my pocket, and an "Albert tie" and a false collar from my neck, while I was helping him over the wall; got reprimanded by the Chief, but not discharged.

Next day saw a row; knew my duty perfectly

well in this instance. Turned down the nearest street and went into a rum-shop; man followed me in, and, as I was taking a "brandy-smash," he stepped up and asked me my name; told him none of his business; asked me again; told him if he didn't shut up I'd break his mouth.

He went off, and I returned to the field of battle and took into custody a man with his head cut open, who was lying across the curb-stone; led him to the Station House, and complained of him for breaking the peace.

Next day was summoned before the Mayor; thought I was going to receive a public compliment for doing my duty, and perhaps get promoted—have my salary raised—and presented with a medal.

Had never seen the Mayor; went into the room, and saw, sitting in the big chair, the man who had asked me the day before what my name was, whose mouth I had threatened to break, and who I now discovered was Mayor Wood.

He asked me my name; didn't say anything about breaking his mouth *this* time; he informed me that the city had no further occasion for my services; hadn't any thing to say; took off my star, gave up my club, and left the presence, resolved that if another man asks my name, to tell him politely,

Q. K. Philander Doesticks, P. B.

P. S.—I have just got a note, saying that my back salary will not be paid. Shall sue the city, for I know that in the fighting business I did my duty as an M. P. according to police usage from time immemorial.

What right has Mayor Wood to come in and upset ancient customs with his new-fangled notions? He may go to thunder.

## XXXIII.

### Damphool Defunct—Place of his Exile—Description thereof—and Exit.

SORROW is upon the heart, a heavy grief upon the soul, and a great affliction in the home of me, Doesticks. My friend, the charm of my chamber, the comforter of my lonely hours, the treasure of my heart, the light of my eyes, the sunshine of my existence, the borrower of my clean shirts and my Sunday pantaloons, the permanent clothing and fancy goods debtor of my life, is no more.

My sack-cloth garment is not as yet complete, my tailor having disappointed me; but dust and ashes lie in alternate strata, undisturbed upon the head of me, Doesticks.

Weep with me, sympathizing world; bear a helping hand to lift away this heavy load of sorrowful sorrow, of woeful woe, of bitter bitterness, of agonizing agony, of wretched wretchedness, and torturing torture, which now afflicts with its direful weight the head of me, Doesticks.

I grieve, I mourn, I lament, I weep, I suffer, I pine, I droop, I sink, I despair, I writhe in agony, I feel bad.

*Damphool* has departed this life.

He is buried, but he is not dead; he is entombed, but he is still alive. After a metropolitan existence of a few months had partially relieved him of his rural verdure; after having seen with appreciating eyes the suburbs of a town which alone contains the entire and undivided *elephant*, he has voluntarily exiled himself to a stagnant village in the Western wilderness—a sleepily-ambitious little townlet, vainly, for many years, aspiring to the dignity of cityhood, but which still remains a very baby of a city, not yet (metaphorically speaking) divested of those rudimentary triangular garments peculiar to weaklings in an undeveloped state—without energy enough to cry when it is hurt, or go-aheadism sufficient to keep its nose clear

A somnambulistic town—for in spite of all the efforts made for its glorification, it has obstinately refused to shake off its municipal drowsiness.

A very Rip Van Winkle of a town, now in the midst of its twenty years' nap, and which will arouse some time and find itself so dilapidated that its former friends won't recognize it.

A town which actualizes that ancient fable of the hare and tortoise—and, trusting in its capability of speed, has gone fast asleep at the beginning of the course, only to awake some future day to the fact that all its tortoise neighbors have passed it on the way, and it has been distanced in the race, rather than be disturbed in its comfortable snooze.

A very sepulchre of a town, into which, if a would-be voyager in the stream of earnest life be cast away and stranded, he is as much lost to the really *living* world, as if he were embalmed with oriental spices, and shelved away in the darkest tomb of the Pharaohs.

A town whose future greatness exists only in the imagination of its deluded habiters, whose enterprise and public spirit are as fabulous as the Phœnix.

A town which will never be a city, save in name, until telegraphs, railroads, colleges, churches, libraries, and busy warehouses become indigenous to the soil of the Wolverines, and spring like mushrooms from the earth, without the aid of human mind to plan, or human will to urge the work, or human hand to place one single stone.

For, sooner than this dormant town shall be matured into a flourishing city by the men who now doze away their time within its sleepy limits, the dead men of Greenwood shall rise from their mossy graves and pile their marble monuments into a tradesman's market-house.

A town, where, in former days, some few short-sighted business men did congregate, who commenced great stores, hotels and warehouses, and the other tools by help of which the world does "*business*," but which said men, too wise to remain faithful to a place which all their toil would ever fail to permanently rouse from its persevering sleep, soon left for ever, after, by united effort, they had galvanized it into a spasmodic life, and taken advantage of its transient vitality to hastily sell their property, before its slumber should come on again. These men are now remembered by the great hotel their enterprise erected, and which is to this day unfi nished, and the warehouses (now deserted, save by rats,) which they put up, and the other massive structure, the work on which was going bravely on, until the drowsy genius of the place congealed the energy of the founders, and left the unroofed walls and rotting timbers a crumbling landmark in the desolate dearth, to show where another business man was wrecked.

A rusty village which has not enterprise enough to keep its public buildings in repair, and whose very Court-house, now in the last decrepit years of a slothful life, has for years leaked dirty water on the heads of the sleepy lawyers who burrow in its dingy lower rooms; and which, in a soaking rain, could not boast a dry corner to protect the dignified caput of the supreme judge from the aqueous visitation.

A town where every one is poorer than his neighbor, and no one man is rich in this world's goods, save those few treacherous pilots, who, being charged to guide the vessels of their fellows, have placed false lights on hidden rocks, run the confiding craft to ruin, and fattened on the plunder of the wreck.

A distant and remote extreme of the hurrying world, which is so separated from the "heart of business" that no single drop of its vital life ever reaches this defunct and amputated member.

A place where the inactivity and inertia of the people infects even the animal and vegetable worlds; and the cows and pigs are too lazy to eat enough to ensure their pinguitude, but drawl about the streets, perambulating specimens of embodied animated laziness, displaying through their skins their osseous economy.

Where the very trees don't leaf out till August and the flowers are too backward to bloom till snow comes, and where the river itself, too lazy to run down hill, sometimes from sheer indolence stops flowing, to take a rest; dams itself up, and overflows the railroad.

Yet here has the late lamented Damphool resolved to bury himself, establishing thereby an undisputed title to the expressive name he bears; and I can only hope that in his exile some stray copy of this book may be wrecked within his reach, that he may come to know the present heartfelt lament of me, Doesticks.

I have ever tried, O mighty Damphool, to forgive thy faults and overlook thy frailties!

Some have said that thou wert lazy, but such have never seen thee eat.

What though thou wert foppish to a degree.

I could forgive thy Shanghae coats, thy two-acre turn-down collars, and thy pantaloons so tight thou hadst to pull them on with boot-hooks; thy gorgeous cravat, with its bow projecting on either side like a silken wing; thy lemon-colored kids; thy cambric handkerchiefs, dripping with compounds to me unknown; and thy blanket shawl, which made thee resemble a half-breed Scotchman.

I could overlook the boarding-school-ism of the Miss Nancyish "Journal," filled with poetry rejected of the press, with unmeaning prose, with dyspeptic complaints of hard fortune, or bilious repinings at thy lot, and all the senseless silliness which thou didst inscribe therein.

I could endure the affected airs thou didst assume before the lady boarders, that they might think and call thee *Poet;* the abstracted air, the appearance of being lost in thought, and the sudden recovery of thy truant wits with a spasmodic start; the shirt-collar loose at the neck, and turned romantically down over the coat; the long hair brushed back behind thy noticeable ears, to show thy "marble forehead."

I could admire that self-appreciation of personal charms which made thee certain all the young ladies were smitten unto matrimony with thy fascinations.

How faithful wert thou in thy gastronomical affections! how constant to thy first love—fried oysters;

and how attentive to the choice of thy mature judgment—boiled turkey, with celery.

How unwavering in thy economy, never parting with a dime in charity, in generosity, or in friendly gift, but only disbursing the same for a full equivalent in the wherewithal to decorate the outer man, or gratify the inner individual.

How consistent in thy devotion to music and the drama; always attending the opera or theatre whenever generous friends would buy the tickets.

What an intense appreciation hadst thou of literature, always going fast asleep over anything more substantial than the morning paper. How fashionably sincere in all thy professions of piety, attending church on Sunday, reading the responses when they could be easily found, and sleeping through the sermon with as much respectability as any Church member of them all; truly, most estimable Damphool, I shall greatly miss thy intermittent religion.

How lovely wert thou in disposition, how amiable in manners; with what an affectionate air couldst thou kick the match-boy out doors, box the ears of the little candy-girl, and tell the more sturdy apple-woman to go to the devil.

With what a charitable look couldst thou listen to

the tale of the shivering beggar child, could see the bare blue feet, and view the scanty dress, while thy generous hand closed with a tighter grasp upon the cherished pennies in thy pocket.

Anatomically speaking, friend Damphool, I suppose thou hadst a heart; emotionally, not a trace of one; the feeble article which served thee in that capacity knew no more of generous thoughts and noble impulses than a Shanghae pullet knows of the opera of Norma.

Go, immerse thyself in that Western town where, like the rest who dwell therein, thy abilities will be undeveloped, thy talents will be veiled, thy energies rust out, and thou wilt become, like them, a perambulating, passive, perpetual sacrifice to the lazy gods of Sloth and Sanctity.

I shall mourn thy taper legs; I shall lament thy excruciating neck-tie; I shall weep that last coat that did so very long a tail unfold; I shall sorrow for thy unctuous hairs, and grieve for thy perfumed whiskers.

I shall look in vain for thy polished boots and jeweled hands; I shall miss thy intellectual countenance, radiant with innocent imbecility; and I shall lose my daily meditation upon the precarious frailty of those intangible legs.

But, ancient friend, when hereafter all the rustic maidens have yielded their hearts before thy captivating charms; when thy manly beauty is fully appreciated, and thy intellectual endowments acknowledged by the world, deign to cast one condescending glance downward toward thy former friend and perpetual admirer, and give one gracious thought of kind remembrance to sorrowing, disconsolate me, Doesticks.

Damphool, thou art superlative—there is none greater.

Farewell! Henceforth, friendship to me is but a name, and I survive my bereavement only to concentrate my affections upon my embryonic whiskers. I remain inconsolable, till the bell rings for dinner.

The Wine Cellar near Cincinnati.

## XXXIV.

### Keeping the Maine Law.

BY the enduring perseverance of the lovers of cold water, laws have been passed in most of the Western States forbidding the sale of those beverages which make men rich, happy, dizzy, and drunk, all in the space of half an hour; so that now a good horn is not, as formerly, to be purchased at every corner grocery, and travellers are forced to carry a couple of "drunks" in a willow-covered flask in their overcoat pocket.

The usual "bitters" are not forthcoming in the morning, and old topers who have for years regularly paid their morning devotions to the decanter or the black bottle, must now perforce become votaries of the hydrant and the rain water barrel.

Not a few men have, within the last four months, drunk more water than for years before, to the great astonishment of their stomachs, which would, at first, almost rebel against the unusual visitor.

Many an habitual guzzler whose convivial habits have generally sent him to bed at five o'clock every afternoon, has been amazed to discover what a difference the new drink makes in the stability of the village constituents; and it will be a matter of wonder to find that at four in the afternoon the town is in comparatively the same situation it was in the morning; that the tavern sign is *not* over the shoemaker's shop, nor the horse-trough in the front-parlor; that the pump is in the street instead of the church belfry, the confectioner's shop *not* in the livery stable, the livery horses *not* in the bakery, the bakery *not* a hardware store, the hardware store *not* full of shingles and building stuff; that the poplar-trees in front of the minister's house are right end up, and the flower-garden of the minister's wife is in a state of ordinary propriety, with no snow-balls growing on the strawberry vines, or strawberries on the lilacs; no blue-bells on the locust-trees, violets on the currant bushes, or lilies in the onion-beds; that there are no tulips on the pickets, and no moss-rose buds springing from the shed,—and that the boy who waters the stage-coach horses every afternoon as the clock strikes quarter to five, does *not* lead them tail first up the church lightning rod, and make them drink from the ridge-pole, as he had always thought.

In short he finds a serious and sudden change in the world around him, and that all the curious phenomena before mentioned and which formerly were always present in the afternoon to his confused vision, immediately after imbibing his seventeenth glass of rum and water, have ceased to occur, and that every thing is now right side up, and front end foremost to his ever before bewildered optics.

And not a few men who would be ashamed to own that they really care anything for the drop of spirits which they occasionally take for the "stomach's sake" will be seriously incommoded by this new stringency in temperance principles; and the deacon or elder who in the privacy of his closet kept a spiritual comforter of half pint dimension will miss, more seriously than he would like to own, even to himself, this pious dram.

Longer faces and sourer tempers will be the result, and many a young aspirant to church membership will be found deficient in necessary Christian graces, which the charitable eyes of his thirsty examiners might have found in abundance, had not the Maine Law interfered with the generosity of their judgment, and made their vision less clear than usual.

But these are things it will not do to speak of; only the gross appetites of the three cent drinker should be made matters of common conversation.

Travelling lately through the thirsty State of Ohio, I had many opportunities of observing how they get round and over the letter of the Law.

In that state the framers of the law, with a commendable regard for the commercial welfare of their constituents, many of whom are large vine-growers, inserted a special clause allowing the traffic in beer and native wine to remain unmolested.

Travellers will therefore find in this State now a greater variety of wine than is grown in any other one country in the world.

Liquors which he, in another place, would recognise as brandy, rum, or gin, are partially disguised under transparent cognomens as native wine.

Brandy-"smashes," rum-punches, gin-cock-tails, sherry-cobblers, mint-juleps, and every kind of desirable potable, are all manufactured from "Longworth's Sparkling"—old corn-whiskey is known as "Still

Catawba"—and a vast deal of the "lager-beer" is put up in brandy casks, and tastes exceedingly like the genuine article.

Being in the vicinity of the Pork city (where they have a ham on the top of the tallest church spire in the place, pointing with the knuckle end to Heaven,) I had an opportunity to visit a large wine-cellar which belonged to Damphool's uncle, who was to accompany us, and had also from him permission to taste the different vintages.

Got to the place, went down cellar, boy gave each of us a long stick with a tallow candle on the end; got down; wine everywhere, in big casks, in long bottles, in small bottles, in tin dippers, in glass vials, and in little puddles on the floor.

Bottles ranged in regiments all wrong side up with cobwebs on the corks.

Every one had the year of the vintage painted on the bottom, as if it was a British baby and its age had to be registered by the parish.

One cask was big enough to float a scow-boat or hold a common-sized church if the steeple wasn't too tall.

Damphool senior wanted to get in and swim—

was afraid he'd get corned and couldn't get out, wouldn't let him try.

He would insist on getting on top of the reservoir - had a glass pump in his hand—pumped up wine for every body—put the spout into his mouth, and pumped into himself for an hour,—first fifteen minutes made him rich; second quarter of an hour made him tearful; at the end of forty-five minutes he was helpless but happy; and when the hour was up he tumbled off the top of the machine and we stowed him away in a corner, where he lay until he revived sufficiently to be able to partake of some bread and butter which the Dutch housekeeper gave us, and which he insisted was lobster salad, and kept calling for boiled eggs, olive oil, and mustard to dress it with.

At last he was taken violently sick, and we took him out doors, set him on top of a basswood stump, when he looked like "Patience on a monument smiling"—although he tried to convince us that he was D. Webster, Esq., and insisted on making a speech to convince us that he "still lived."

Never before had I seen wine of such tremendous power. One of our party was addressing a number of pint bottles alternately as "Fellow citizens," 'Gentlemen of the Jury," and "Ladies of the Committee."

Another had seated himself in a small puddle of Still Catawba on the brick floor, and was calling out for soap, towels, and a black boy to scrub his shoulders.

A third had emptied four bottles of "sparkling" into his vest-pockets to take home to the children, and put the fragments of the glass into his hat under the impression that they were hickory nuts, which he tried to crack with the carriage lamps, evidently supposing them to be nut-crackers.

My most intimate friend was trying to feed the horse some oats, by which appellation he called a three-cornered harrow and a breaking-up plough, and had filled the buggy with wild flowers, as he supposed, but which were, in reality, two year old grape vines, which he had pulled up by the roots.

Did not allow myself to become affected in like manner, as I had to spend the evening with the family of one of the "solid men" of Porkopolis, an ardent supporter of the Maine Law, who always keeps a large variety of liquors in his cellars, and insists, whenever his friends spend an evening with him, on making them pass their time drinking whiskey-punch, with seven whiskeys to one water. Passed a delightful evening, called the children by French names, mistook the piano for the hat-rack, hung my hat on the harp-pedal, and laid my gloves on the key-board. Met Damphool's uncle as I was going to the hotel; he had brought home the glass-pump, thinking it was our carriage-whip, but was otherwise sensible.

Is going to sell his vineyard, and turn teetotaler.

## XXXV.

### Theatricals once more.—Shakspeare darkeyized.—Macbeth in high colors.

IN a street of the city, not more than four miles from the City Hall, in humble imitation of the magnificent temples of the Drama erected by ambitious managers in more pretentious portions of the town, the sable portion of our population have also built an appropriate mansion wherein is supposed to reside the dingy Genius of Ebony Theatricals.

A portrait of some sable Garrick adorns the drop curtain; a thick-lipped lady of dark complexion on one side of the proscenium represents the Goddess of Tragedy; and on the other a woolly-headed brunette in short skirts is supposed to stand for the Goddess of Comedy.

What though the portrait of the African Roscius in the drop centre, instead of Classic Roman robes, is attired in a swallow-tailed coat, with brass buttons and a red velvet collar? and what if the two ladies before mentioned are resplendent in sky-blue dresses and yellow turbans? perhaps their unusual garb is quite as appropriate to the atmosphere of the place, as the more elaborate, more classic, more costly, but considerably less gaudy wardrobe allotted to corresponding divinities in more fashionable Theatres.

The appointments generally at this place might not be considered very tasteful by the "white trash," who get their ideas of propriety from Wallack's or Burton's; but any impartial observer will admit that the scenery is more creditable than the dirty green and brick-red abomination of the Metropolitan, or the paint and canvas hash with Dutch metal seasoning, which has been for years a standing dish at the Broadway, and which is still served up nightly to a surfeited audience.

The female visitors who attend the delectable performances of the talented corps of this colored establishment, do not make themselves quite so ridiculous with their dress as their white competitors, but it is only because they have not the money to be as fashionable; the desire is probably fully as strong, but the cash don't hold out.

And as the white folks, in the construction of their pieces for dramatic representation, sometimes represent in a peculiar light the warmer blooded passions of their "dark complected" neighbors, in retaliation the colored dramatists reverse the order and make the white men in their drama wait upon the colored heroes, black their boots, groom their imaginary horses, brush their coats, and perform all the varied round of servile duties which in representatives of the same plays by white men are assigned to them.

The play of Othello is the single exception—they make the Venetian warrior a white man in a red roundabout, who makes fierce love to Desdemona, who is the molasses-colored child of a respectable darkey whitewasher.

Lorgnettes, Opera-hoods, and white kids are not exhibited here in such profusion as in some other places of amusement; on the contrary, green spectacles, sun-bonnets, and calico dresses are rather in the ascendant.

As a phase of city life which does not often turn its side to the public, and as a place to enjoy an unlimited amount of fun for a little money, the Church street colored Theatre is well worth visiting.

A grand Shakspearean festival was lately announced to come off here, on which occasion the tragedy of Macbeth was to be performed with "all the original music, new and gorgeous scenery, rich and elegant costumes, magnificent scenic appointments, &c.," according to the time-honored "gag" in such case made and provided.

The novelty of seeing a black Macbeth with the entire tragedy done in colors by the best artists, promised to be almost as good a burlesque as the bearded Indian exhibition made by the great American Tragedian at the Broadway; and so with a varied assortment of friends I started to witness the unusual spectacle of a Bowery darkey representing a Scotch king.

Paid the entrance fee all in dimes, as the door-keeper couldn't read the Counterfeit Detector, and wouldn't take bills for fear he would get stuck with bad money.

Orchestra consisted of a bass-drum, one violin, and a cornet-à-piston. Seats, new benches with coffee-sacks spread over those constituting the Dress Circle.

Orchestra essayed the Prima Donna Waltz, which gradually degenerated into "Wait for the Wagon," and concluded in "Few Days."

Great deal of whispering and shuffling about behind the scenes, a great deal of emphatic ordering about from the unseen prompter, who was trying, as nearly as I could judge, to have Macduff take his chew of tobacco out of his mouth, and at last the curtain rolled up.

Macbeth was a fat gentleman of jetty hue who might have been head-cook at Delmonico's for twenty years, and who would, had he been subjected to a melting process, have furnished soap and candles enough for a small chandlery business.

Whether he *intended* to give the tragedy a gastronomical interpretation or not is uncertain, but it is a veritable fact that he dressed the character in a cook's apron, had a paper cap with a long turkey feather in it on his head, his steel by his side, a butcher-knife in his hand, and the cover of the soup-pot for a shield.

Macduff was attired more like a Lake Superior Indian than anything else, with a superfluity of red flannel fringe, and silver rings in his ears and nose.

Lady Macbeth rejoiced in a tin crown with seven points, each one with a crescent on top, brass-heeled gaiters, a dress with a purple waist, and a green baize train, two cameo bracelets, and lemon-colored kid gloves.

Old King Duncan was a young man who seemed to labor under the impression that to support his royal dignity it was only necessary to grin incessantly, and turn his toes in when he walked; his royal highness had on a high hat with a red feather, plaid pantaloons (being the only symptom of Scotch costume visible during the evening), and an embroidered vest, through which, as he wore no coat, the sleeves of his blue shirt appeared in agreeable contrast; he sported a silver watch, four seal rings, an opera glass, and a gold-headed cane.

All the other characters were dressed with equal regard to propriety and elegance of costume, and with equal *dis*regard to expense.

The warlike paraphernalia were on the same appropriate scale; instead of Scottish claymores and basket-hilted swords, muskets were introduced which had probably seen service in some target company, until too battered and damaged for further use; shields were dispensed with except in the single case of Macduff,—instead of daggers, many were provided with horse-pistols, and one aspiring individual had a sword-cane and a slung-shot.

Several of the "supes" were painted like Indians, and carried banners made of horse-blankets, nailed to barrel staves—the three witches had each a hoe and a stable-fork, and Hecate was equipped with a straw-hat and a pair of linen drawers put on hind-side foremost.

The play commenced, and every thing proceeded in the greatest harmony until the caldron scene, when the apparitions, instead of rising through the trap into the caldron, deliberately crawled from the ring on their hands and knees, and stuck their heads through a hole in a board which was painted in admirable imitation of a dinnerpot, and delivered their prophetic speeches in a huge whisper to the anxious Thane.

The apparition of a "child's head crowned," as the stage direction reads, was done by a fat piccaninny, who was drawn on screaming and kicking in a willow basket by a hidden rope, and the speech was read by the prompter, who squatted down behind the basket, and held his hand over the baby's mouth in a vain effort to stop his noise.

During this scene Macbeth, who was too obese to stand for so long a time comfortably, seated himself composedly on a three-legged stool which did duty afterwards as a throne,—and in fact, whenever during the performance he found himself incommoded by the warmth, he would sit flat down on the most convenient resting-place.

His rendering of the dagger scene was peculiarly original—he took his butcher-knife, tied it by a tow string to a pitch-fork which he stuck in the middle of the stage, sat flat down on the floor before it, and proceeded to deliver the speech with great force and emotion; pausing occasionally to mop his forehead with a yellow bandana handkerchief, and refresh himself by long sips from a pewter mug of beer which he had bestowed in his original shield.

The rest of the company got along very well, managing the removal of Birnam wood in rather a unique manner—when the soldier spoke of a "moving wood" a back scene opened and discovered four darkies carrying pine kindling wood from a wagon with a jackass team, down cellar into a coal-hole.

Whenever an actor forgot his part the prompter would rush out from his hiding place, put the offending artist in the proper position, read his lines for him, and suddenly disappear, until some fresh delinquency called for another shirt-sleeve advent.

Matters progressed towards the close of the piece —Lady Macbeth had played the lighted candle scene (using a bed-lamp, a candle not being forthcoming)—had made her last exit, leaving the green baize train, which had come untied, in the middle of the stage, a sad memorial of her fate—the soldiers had met in a pitched battle (every "Supe" had insisted on dying a death of his own, in order to display his tragic genius), and had expired in various uncomfortable positions; one sitting up against the flat, with his leg through a trap-door, and his mouth open, and another with his head through a bushel basket which he had brought on to use as a shield—all the minor business of the piece was got along with, and it only remained for Macduff and the rotund Macbeth to have their fight, say their say, die their die, and finish the play.

They entered arm in arm, being evidently determined, like prize-fighters, to do their "bloody business" amicably, and as old friends ought.

Macduff remarked to the audience that they were going to "settle that little quarrel"—they then proceeded to strip for the contest.

Macduff retired to one corner and pulled off his boots and spectacles, Macbeth went to another and laid down his jacket and shield—then they met in the middle, shook hands—one flourished a long toasting-fork—the other wielded a rolling-pin—Macbeth made the last speech as follows—

"Come on!!! Macduff be damned!!!" both pitched in—first round, toasting-fork ahead, rolling-pin in the corner with his nose bloody—second round, toasting-fork knocks rolling-pin through a parlor scene and falls back exhausted—third round, both come to time with difficulty, toaster hits roller in the stomach, roller shies his weapon at toaster's head, toaster spears at roller's toes, and breaks his fork.

All their munitions of war being exhausted, they close in an expiring wrestle, and Macbeth eventually dies, having first in the terrific struggle suffered amputation of the pantaloons immediately above both knees.

Macduff recovers his rolling-pin, and stands over the conquered Macbeth in a grand saw-buck attitude of victory and triumph.

## XXXVI.

### Young America in Long Dresses—Great Excitement in Babydom.

THE late grand convention of precocious and pinguid children, created such a stir throughout the country, that the news, by some unknown conveyance, penetrated even to the obscure Wolverine hamlet wherein Damphool had for four months been content to vegetate. The infantile humbug promised something new in the way of sight-seeing, and as he desired to meet all his relatives and namesakes who would be certain to be present on that eventful occasion, and wished to improve this noble opportunity of contemplating the infant Damphools of the country, who were to be there exhibited by their stultified progenitors, he took the next train of cars and started for Gotham, to view this first congress of rudimentary "humans."

His immediate care, on reaching the city, was to

repair to the establishment where I, his former friend, am generally to be found,—having discovered the object of his search, he had some considerable difficulty in convincing me of the utility of such a show, or the absolute necessity that existed of visiting such a promiscuous assemblage of everybody's brats; and paying twenty-five cents to hear a squalling chorus by the unregulated voices of the young ones, and to view the prolific women who had so increased the population of the country, in some cases by as many as four at a single litter.

I had some old fashioned notions that babies should be kept at home, and allowed to take their necessary allowance of nutriment, and soil their *un*-necessary allowance of linen (a baby is always wrapped up in cloth enough to full-rig a topsail schooner, from the middle of which its insignificant head sticks out, like a lap-dog which has been rolled up by mistake in the parlor carpet), within the limits of the domestic circle; and not paraded before the public to perform these pleasing functions in the presence of an assemblage, composed in great part, of modest young men and bashful maidens, uninitiated as yet, in the mysteries of baby life.

After laboring for some time to convince me that

adolescent and embryo human stock is as legitimate a subject of exhibition as any other animals, and that fecund mothers and high-blooded fathers should be as much brought into public notice as brood mares, or imported Durham cattle; and that public displays of fine children, and a discussion of the mode of rearing and training them, and an interchange of sentiments on these important points between those of most experience in the matter, would tend to the great physical improvement of the human race, I was so far satisfied that I agreed to go and witness the latest effort of the "Great American Showman" to get up a sensation.

Went to the entrance of the place of exhibition, took a look at the show-bills below, and the huge painting above, which represented in the most prominent rainbow hues the supposed appearance of the infant wonders—at the waxen boy in a scratch wig and full suit of Young America clothes, and the impassible girl of like material, whose Cereous head was covered with such a crop of hempen curls that if woven into a rope it would have been long enough to hang half the rogues in the city; which two infant prodigies were the contribution of some enterprising hair-dresser and wig-maker, and were most industriously revolving beneath two glass cases in the hall in front of the paying place, and whose striking beauty was presumed to be all-powerful to arrest the attention of the hurrying multitude and make them lay down their quarters and take a peep at the exhibition whether they would or no ; having, I say, taken a bird's eye glance at all these, we laid down our money (Damphool paid for both) and entered.

Tremendous crowd—hurried in—got my toes annihilated, my hat smashed in, and my shirt collar reduced to the dimensions and appearance of a slimy dishcloth, in less than a minute.

Forced our way up to the platform. Saw a number of complacent mothers with movable fronts to their dresses, sitting side by side on an elevated plank, holding their babies in their laps (each one having a stock of baby linen handy, and a huge bucket of some liquid to me unknown, but which looked like starch, within reach, and which every now and then they poured into the faces of the specimen babies who lay with their wide mouths open like so many young robins) casting jealous glances at each other, tender glances on their young charges, and appealing glances at the crowd before them.

The youngest babies were dressed in unaccustomed clean clothes, in which, as they were unused to such style of garments, they looked ten times dirtier than ever—they had a profusion of green and blue ribbons on their frocks, which they kept in their mouths all the time—their faces were full of wrinkles, their eyes were watery and weak, and their pug-noses seemed to be living fountains.

Other babies under the required age (4 years), decked out in all sorts of colors, and with dresses made universally in most execrably bad taste, were standing on some of the other platforms, or running about amongst the crowd, daubing themselves and those indiscreet and enthusiastic persons who attempted to handle them, with half-dissolved candy, and sticky gingerbread. And occasionally getting up a fight among themselves—where little fists would unceremoniously visit little eyes, and little feet would indulge in a series of energetic little kicks, and little fingers would pull out little bunches of little curls, and little voices would give a course of most discordant screams (which were *little*, but ——), and so the little Tom Hyers would amuse themselves until separated by some courageous individual who dared to touch the little monsters.

I stepped up to a lady to ask the age of a baby which she had in her maternal arms, when I found myself instantly a centre of baby attraction—babies seemed to pitch into me from all directions—a baby poked its fingers into my eye, a baby put sugar on my ruffled shirt, a baby daubed gruel on my white vest, a baby filled my kid glove with milk, a baby dropped something done up in a rag down my neck, and a baby of huge dimensions and unredeemed ugliness amused itself by filling my hat full of playthings which it appropriated from the weaker babies on either side. So that I found in that article of apparel a tin whistle, three dolls, a sugar house, a miniature Noah's Ark with all the animals, a rattle-box, a hair-brush, and two india-rubber balls.

Tried to get out of the muss, but a baby was pulling my coat-tails, and a four-year old baby stood upon each foot improving the pattern of my white pants by wiping their dirty hands thereon. I stepped back and knocked over a baby, I rushed forward and stepped on a baby, I leaped to one side and crushed a small baby in a pink dress, I sprung to the other and crushed a fat baby and its nurse against the wall. I tried to escape from the room but tumbled over a baby,—recovered my feet and started again, but babies got between my legs and tripped me down-stairs, where I landed in an exhausted condition, which was by no means im proved by a careless woman dropping her baby directly on my head from the fourth-story.

Saw the distribution of prizes,—first prize given to an Irish baby with a stub nose; second, to a Dutch ditto, with eyes of different colors; and all the rest to the very babies who ought not to have had any, but deserved to be spanked and sent to bed until they should grow decent looking.

Not a good-looking baby got a prize, and the very ones who should have taken the premiums were sent home without having their expenses paid.

The $100 prize baby did not amount to much after all. Not a young couple who saw it but thought they could do better in less than a year; and the mothers of those babies who didn't get anything thought they could beat it on six months' notice.

Those industrious ladies who desired tc rear a large family in the shortest time possible, and so had produced three or four children at a birth, were all rewarded by the Great Showman for their extra pains and labors, and all went home triumphant with a premium for fecundity, and money enough to buy flannel for all the brood.

Everybody said the baby show was a humbug—but everybody went to see it. Everybody said it was disgusting, but everybody paid his twenty-five cents to be disgusted, and everybody *was* disgusted to his heart's content.

No one was perfectly satisfied except the mothers of the lucky babies, and the proprietor of the entire concern, who made a small fortune by the operation.

The excitement is now over, the public have seen the sight, the press has had its say, the women have shown their babies, Damphool has gone back to the country, and the world is once more comparatively quiet.

No other so great excitement will agitate the world until next year, when the Great Showman intends to revive the subject, and show the world the modus operandi of baby birth, with illustrations by the mothers of the babies who took the prizes this year, and who in another twelve-month will probably have no shame at all in the matter, and will stick at nothing. Let us wait, and hope.

www.ingramcontent.com/pod-product-compliance
Lightning Source LLC
LaVergne TN
LVHW020214110826
845151LV00003B/713

* 9 7 8 1 4 2 5 5 3 3 6 4 9 *